HIS MAJESTY THE KING OF THE BELGIANS,

HER MAJESTY THE QUEEN OF DENMARK,

THE PRESIDENT OF THE FEDERAL REPUBLIC OF GERMANY,

THE PRESIDENT OF THE HELLENIC REPUBLIC,

HIS MAJESTY THE KING OF SPAIN,

THE PRESIDENT OF THE FRENCH REPUBLIC,

THE PRESIDENT OF IRELAND,

THE PRESIDENT OF THE ITALIAN REPUBLIC,

HIS ROYAL HIGHNESS THE GRAND DUKE OF LUXEMBOURG,

HER MAJESTY THE QUEEN OF THE NETHERLANDS,

THE PRESIDENT OF THE PORTUGUESE REPUBLIC,

HER MAJESTY THE QUEEN OF THE UNITED KINGDOM OF GREAT BRITAIN AND NORTHERN IRELAND,

RESOLVED to mark a new stage in the process of European integration undertaken with the establishment of the European Communities,

RECALLING the historic importance of the ending of the division of the European continent and the need to create firm bases for the construction of the future Europe,

CONFIRMING their attachment to the principles of liberty, democracy and respect for human rights and fundamental freedoms and of the rule of law,

DESIRING to deepen the solidarity between their peoples while respecting their history, their culture and their traditions,

DESIRING to enhance further the democratic and efficient functioning of the institutions so as to enable them better to carry out, within a single institutional framework, the tasks entrusted to them,

RESOLVED to achieve the strengthening and the convergence of their economies and to establish an economic and monetary union including, in accordance with the provisions of this Treaty, a single and stable currency,

DETERMINED to promote economic and social progress for their peoples, within the context of the accomplishment of the internal market and of reinforced cohesion and environmental protection, and to implement policies ensuring that advances in economic integration are accompanied by parallel progress in other fields,

RESOLVED to establish a citizenship common to nationals of their countries,

RESOLVED to implement a common foreign and security policy including the eventual framing of a common defence policy, which might in time lead to a common defence, thereby reinforcing the European identity and its independence in order to promote peace, security and progress in Europe and in the world,

REAFFIRMING their objective to facilitate the free movement of persons, while ensuring the safety and security of their peoples, by including provisions on justice and home affairs in this Treaty,

RESOLVED to continue the process of creating an ever closer union among the peoples of Europe, in which decisions are taken as closely as possible to the citizen in accordance with the principle of subsidiarity,

IN VIEW of further steps to be taken in order to advance European integration,

HAVE DECIDED to establish a European Union and to this end have designated as their plenipotentiaries:

HIS MAJESTY THE KING OF THE BELGIANS:

Mark EYSKENS,
Minister for Foreign Affairs;

Philippe MAYSTADT,
Minister for Finance;

HER MAJESTY THE QUEEN OF DENMARK:

Uffe ELLEMANN-JENSEN,
Minister for Foreign Affairs;

Anders FOGH RASMUSSEN,
Minister for Economic Affairs;

THE PRESIDENT OF THE FEDERAL REPUBLIC OF GERMANY:

Hans-Dietrich GENSCHER,
Federal Minister for Foreign Affairs;

Theodor WAIGEL,
Federal Minister for Finance;

THE PRESIDENT OF THE HELLENIC REPUBLIC:

Antonios SAMARAS,
Minister for Foreign Affairs;

Efthymios CHRISTODOULOU,
Minister for Economic Affairs;

HIS MAJESTY THE KING OF SPAIN:

Francisco FERNÁNDEZ ORDÓÑEZ,
Minister for Foreign Affairs;

Carlos SOLCHAGA CATALÁN,
Minister for Economic Affairs and Finance;

THE PRESIDENT OF THE FRENCH REPUBLIC:

Roland DUMAS,
Minister for Foreign Affairs;

Pierre BEREGOVOY,
Minister for Economic and Financial Affairs and the Budget;

THE PRESIDENT OF IRELAND:

Gerard COLLINS,
Minister for Foreign Affairs;

Bertie AHERN,
Minister for Finance;

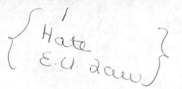

THE PRESIDENT OF THE ITALIAN REPUBLIC:

Gianni DE MICHELIS,
Minister for Foreign Affairs;

Guido CARLI,
Minister for the Treasury;

HIS ROYAL HIGHNESS THE GRAND DUKE OF LUXEMBOURG:

Jacques F. POOS,
Deputy Prime Minister,
Minister for Foreign Affairs;

Jean-Claude JUNCKER,
Minister for Finance;

HER MAJESTY THE QUEEN OF THE NETHERLANDS:

Hans van den BROEK,
Minister for Foreign Affairs;

Willem KOK,
Minister for Finance;

THE PRESIDENT OF THE PORTUGUESE REPUBLIC:

João de Deus PINHEIRO,
Minister for Foreign Affairs;

Jorge BRAGA de MACEDO,
Minister for Finance;

HER MAJESTY THE QUEEN OF THE UNITED KINGDOM OF GREAT BRITAIN AND NORTHERN IRELAND:

The Rt. Hon. Douglas HURD,
Secretary of State for Foreign and Commonwealth Affairs;

The Hon. Francis MAUDE,
Financial Secretary to the Treasury;

WHO, having exchanged their full powers, found in good and due form, have agreed as follows.

6

TITLE I

COMMON PROVISIONS

Article A

By this Treaty, the High Contracting Parties establish among themselves a European Union, hereinafter called 'the Union'.

This Treaty marks a new stage in the process of creating an ever closer union among the peoples of Europe, in which decisions are taken as closely as possible to the citizen.

The Union shall be founded on the European Communities, supplemented by the policies and forms of cooperation established by this Treaty. Its task shall be to organize, in a manner demonstrating consistency and solidarity, relations between the Member States and between their peoples.

Article B

The Union shall set itself the following objectives:

— to promote economic and social progress which is balanced and sustainable, in particular through the creation of an area without internal frontiers, through the strengthening of economic and social cohesion and through the establishment of economic and monetary union, ultimately including a single currency in accordance with the provisions of this Treaty;

— to assert its identity on the international scene, in particular through the implementation of a common foreign and security policy including the eventual framing of a common defence policy, which might in time lead to a common defence;

— to strengthen the protection of the rights and interests of the nationals of its Member States through the introduction of a citizenship of the Union;

— to develop close cooperation on justice and home affairs;

— to maintain in full the *acquis communautaire* and build on it with a view to considering, through the procedure referred to in Article N (2), to what extent the policies and forms of cooperation introduced by this Treaty may need to be revised with the aim of ensuring the effectiveness of the mechanisms and the institutions of the Community.

The objectives of the Union shall be achieved as provided in this Treaty and in accordance with the conditions and the timetable set out therein while respecting the principle of subsidiarity as defined in Article 3b of the Treaty establishing the European Community.

Article C

The Union shall be served by a single institutional framework which shall ensure the consistency and the continuity of the activities carried out in order to attain its objectives while respecting and building upon the *acquis communautaire*.

The Union shall in particular ensure the consistency of its external activities as a whole in the context of its external relations, security, economic and development policies. The Council and the Commission shall be responsible for ensuring such consistency. They shall ensure the implementation of these policies, each in accordance with its respective powers.

Article D

The European Council shall provide the Union with the necessary impetus for its development and shall define the general political guidelines thereof.

The European Council shall bring together the Heads of State or Government of the Member States and the President of the Commission. They shall be assisted by the Ministers for Foreign Affairs of the Member States and by a Member of the Commission. The European Council shall meet at least twice a year, under the chairmanship of the Head of State or Government of the Member State which holds the Presidency of the Council.

The European Council shall submit to the European Parliament a report after each of its meetings and a yearly written report on the progress achieved by the Union.

Article E

The European Parliament, the Council, the Commission and the Court of Justice shall exercise their powers under the conditions and for the purposes provided for, on the one hand, by the provisions of the Treaties establishing the European Communities and of the subsequent Treaties and Acts modifying and supplementing them and, on the other hand, by the other provisions of this Treaty.

Article F

1. The Union shall respect the national identities of its Member States, whose systems of government are founded on the principles of democracy.

2. The Union shall respect fundamental rights, as guaranteed by the European Convention for the Protection of Human Rights and Fundamental Freedoms signed in Rome on 4 November 1950 and as they result from the constitutional traditions common to the Member States, as general principles of Community law.

3. The Union shall provide itself with the means necessary to attain its objectives and carry through its policies.

TITLE II

PROVISIONS AMENDING THE TREATY ESTABLISHING THE EUROPEAN ECONOMIC COMMUNITY WITH A VIEW TO ESTABLISHING THE EUROPEAN COMMUNITY

Article G

The Treaty establishing the European Economic Community shall be amended in accordance with the provisions of this Article, in order to establish a European Community.

A — Throughout the Treaty:

(1) The term 'European Economic Community' shall be replaced by the term 'European Community'.

B — In Part One 'Principles':

(2) Article 2 shall be replaced by the following:

'Article 2

The Community shall have as its task, by establishing a common market and an economic and monetary union and by implementing the common policies or activities referred to in Articles 3 and 3a, to promote throughout the Community a harmonious and balanced development of economic activities, sustainable and non-inflationary growth respecting the environment, a high degree of convergence of economic performance, a high level of employment and of social protection, the raising of the standard of living and quality of life, and economic and social cohesion and solidarity among Member States.'

(3) Article 3 shall be replaced by the following:

'*Article 3*

For the purposes set out in Article 2, the activities of the Community shall include, as provided in this Treaty and in accordance with the timetable set out therein:

(a) *the elimination, as between Member States, of customs duties and quantitative restrictions on the import and export of goods, and of all other measures having equivalent effect;*

(b) *a common commercial policy;*

(c) *an internal market characterized by the abolition, as between Member States, of obstacles to the free movement of goods, persons, services and capital;*

(d) *measures concerning the entry and movement of persons in the internal market as provided for in Article 100c;*

(e) *a common policy in the sphere of agriculture and fisheries;*

(f) *a common policy in the sphere of transport;*

(g) *a system ensuring that competition in the internal market is not distorted;*

(h) *the approximation of the laws of Member States to the extent required for the functioning of the common market;*

(i) *a policy in the social sphere comprising a European Social Fund;*

(j) *the strengthening of economic and social cohesion;*

(k) *a policy in the sphere of the environment;*

(l) *the strengthening of the competitiveness of Community industry;*

(m) *the promotion of research and technological development;*

(n) *encouragement for the establishment and development of trans-European networks;*

(o) *a contribution to the attainment of a high level of health protection;*

(p) *a contribution to education and training of quality and to the flowering of the cultures of the Member States;*

(q) a policy in the sphere of development cooperation;

(r) the association of the overseas countries and territories in order to increase trade and promote jointly economic and social development;

(s) a contribution to the strengthening of consumer protection;

(t) measures in the spheres of energy, civil protection and tourism.'

(4) The following Article shall be inserted:

'Article 3a

1. For the purposes set out in Article 2, the activities of the Member States and the Community shall include, as provided in this Treaty and in accordance with the timetable set out therein, the adoption of an economic policy which is based on the close coordination of Member States' economic policies, on the internal market and on the definition of common objectives, and conducted in accordance with the principle of an open market economy with free competition.

2. Concurrently with the foregoing, and as provided in this Treaty and in accordance with the timetable and the procedures set out therein, these activities shall include the irrevocable fixing of exchange rates leading to the introduction of a single currency, the ecu, and the definition and conduct of a single monetary policy and exchange-rate policy the primary objective of both of which shall be to maintain price stability and, without prejudice to this objective, to support the general economic policies in the Community, in accordance with the principle of an open market economy with free competition.

3. These activities of the Member States and the Community shall entail compliance with the following guiding principles: stable prices, sound public finances and monetary conditions and a sustainable balance of payments.'

(5) The following Article shall be inserted:

'Article 3b

The Community shall act within the limits of the powers conferred upon it by this Treaty and of the objectives assigned to it therein.

In areas which do not fall within its exclusive competence, the Community shall take action, in accordance with the principle of subsidiarity, only if and in so far as the objectives of the proposed action cannot be sufficiently achieved by the

Member States and can therefore, by reason of the scale or effects of the proposed action, be better achieved by the Community.

Any action by the Community shall not go beyond what is necessary to achieve the objectives of this Treaty.'

(6) Article 4 shall be replaced by the following:

'Article 4

1. The tasks entrusted to the Community shall be carried out by the following institutions:

— *a EUROPEAN PARLIAMENT,*

— *a COUNCIL,*

— *a COMMISSION,*

— *a COURT OF JUSTICE,*

— *a COURT OF AUDITORS.*

Each institution shall act within the limits of the powers conferred upon it by this Treaty.

2. The Council and the Commission shall be assisted by an Economic and Social Committee and a Committee of the Regions acting in an advisory capacity.'

(7) The following Articles shall be inserted:

'Article 4a

A European System of Central Banks (hereinafter referred to as "ESCB") and a European Central Bank (hereinafter referred to as "ECB") shall be established in accordance with the procedures laid down in this Treaty; they shall act within the limits of the powers conferred upon them by this Treaty and by the Statute of the ESCB and of the ECB (hereinafter referred to as "Statute of the ESCB") annexed thereto.

Article 4b

A European Investment Bank is hereby established, which shall act within the limits of the powers conferred upon it by this Treaty and the Statute annexed thereto.'

(8) Article 6 shall be deleted and Article 7 shall become Article 6. Its second paragraph shall be replaced by the following:

'The Council, acting in accordance with the procedure referred to in Article 189c, may adopt rules designed to prohibit such discrimination.'

(9) Articles 8, 8a, 8b and 8c shall become respectively Articles 7, 7a, 7b and 7c.

C — The following Part shall be inserted:

'PART TWO

CITIZENSHIP OF THE UNION

Article 8

1. Citizenship of the Union is hereby established.

Every person holding the nationality of a Member State shall be a citizen of the Union.

2. Citizens of the Union shall enjoy the rights conferred by this Treaty and shall be subject to the duties imposed thereby. .

Article 8a

1. Every citizen of the Union shall have the right to move and reside freely within the territory of the Member States, subject to the limitations and conditions laid down in this Treaty and by the measures adopted to give it effect.

2. The Council may adopt provisions with a view to facilitating the exercise of the rights referred to in paragraph 1; save as otherwise provided in this Treaty, the Council shall act unanimously on a proposal from the Commission and after obtaining the assent of the European Parliament.

Article 8b

1. Every citizen of the Union residing in a Member State of which he is not a national shall have the right to vote and to stand as a candidate at municipal elections in the Member State in which he resides, under the same conditions as nationals of that State. This right shall be exercised subject to detailed arrangements to be adopted before 31 December 1994 by the Council, acting unanimously on a proposal from the Commission and after consulting the

European Parliament; these arrangements may provide for derogations where warranted by problems specific to a Member State.

2. Without prejudice to Article 138(3) and to the provisions adopted for its implementation, every citizen of the Union residing in a Member State of which he is not a national shall have the right to vote and to stand as a candidate in elections to the European Parliament in the Member State in which he resides, under the same conditions as nationals of that State. This right shall be exercised subject to detailed arrangements to be adopted before 31 December 1993 by the Council, acting unanimously on a proposal from the Commission and after consulting the European Parliament; these arrangements may provide for derogations where warranted by problems specific to a Member State.

Article 8c

Every citizen of the Union shall, in the territory of a third country in which the Member State of which he is a national is not represented, be entitled to protection by the diplomatic or consular authorities of any Member State, on the same conditions as the nationals of that State. Before 31 December 1993, Member States shall establish the necessary rules among themselves and start the international negotiations required to secure this protection.

Article 8d

Every citizen of the Union shall have the right to petition the European Parliament in accordance with Article 138d.

Every citizen of the Union may apply to the Ombudsman established in accordance with Article 138e.

Article 8e

The Commission shall report to the European Parliament, to the Council and to the Economic and Social Committee before 31 December 1993 and then every three years on the application of the provisions of this Part. This report shall take account of the development of the Union.

On this basis, and without prejudice to the other provisions of this Treaty, the Council, acting unanimously on a proposal from the Commission and after consulting the European Parliament, may adopt provisions to strengthen or to add to the rights laid down in this Part, which it shall recommend to the Member States for adoption in accordance with their respective constitutional requirements.'

D — Parts Two and Three shall be grouped under the following Title:

'PART THREE

COMMUNITY POLICIES'

and in this Part:

(10) The first sentence of Article 49 shall be replaced by the following:

'As soon as this Treaty enters into force, the Council shall, acting in accordance with the procedure referred to in Article 189b and after consulting the Economic and Social Committee, issue directives or make regulations setting out the measures required to bring about, by progressive stages, freedom of movement for workers, as defined in Article 48, in particular:'

(11) Article 54(2) shall be replaced by the following:

'2. In order to implement this general programme or, in the absence of such programme, in order to achieve a stage in attaining freedom of establishment as regards a particular activity, the Council, acting in accordance with the procedure referred to in Article 189b and after consulting the Economic and Social Committee, shall act by means of directives.'

(12) Article 56(2) shall be replaced by the following:

'2. Before the end of the transitional period, the Council shall, acting unanimously on a proposal from the Commission and after consulting the European Parliament, issue directives for the coordination of the abovementioned provisions laid down by law, regulation or administrative action. After the end of the second stage, however, the Council shall, acting in accordance with the procedure referred to in Article 189b, issue directives for the coordination of such provisions as, in each Member State, are a matter for regulation or administrative action.'

(13) Article 57 shall be replaced by the following:

'Article 57

1. In order to make it easier for persons to take up and pursue activities as self-employed persons, the Council shall, acting in accordance with the procedure referred to in Article 189b, issue directives for the mutual recognition of diplomas, certificates and other evidence of formal qualifications.

2. *For the same purpose, the Council shall, before the end of the transitional period, issue directives for the coordination of the provisions laid down by law, regulation or administrative action in Member States concerning the taking up and pursuit of activities as self-employed persons. The Council, acting unanimously on a proposal from the Commission and after consulting the European Parliament, shall decide on directives the implementation of which involves in at least one Member State amendment of the existing principles laid down by law governing the professions with respect to training and conditions of access for natural persons. In other cases the Council shall act in accordance with the procedure referred to in Article 189b.*

3. *In the case of the medical and allied and pharmaceutical professions, the progressive abolition of restrictions shall be dependent upon coordination of the conditions for their exercise in the various Member States.'*

(14) The title of Chapter 4 shall be replaced by the following:

'CHAPTER 4

Capital and payments'

(15) The following Articles shall be inserted:

'Article 73a

As from 1 January 1994, Articles 67 to 73 shall be replaced by Articles 73b, c, d, e, f and g.

Article 73b

1. *Within the framework of the provisions set out in this Chapter, all restrictions on the movement of capital between Member States and between Member States and third countries shall be prohibited.*

2. *Within the framework of the provisions set out in this Chapter, all restrictions on payments between Member States and between Member States and third countries shall be prohibited.*

Article 73c

1. *The provisions of Article 73b shall be without prejudice to the application to third countries of any restrictions which exist on 31 December 1993 under national or Community law adopted in respect of the movement of capital to or*

from third countries involving direct investment — including investment in real estate — establishment, the provision of financial services or the admission of securities to capital markets.

2. Whilst endeavouring to achieve the objective of free movement of capital between Member States and third countries to the greatest extent possible and without prejudice to the other Chapters of this Treaty, the Council may, acting by a qualified majority on a proposal from the Commission, adopt measures on the movement of capital to or from third countries involving direct investment — including investment in real estate — establishment, the provision of financial services or the admission of securities to capital markets. Unanimity shall be required for measures under this paragraph which constitute a step back in Community law as regards the liberalization of the movement of capital to or from third countries.

Article 73d

1. The provisions of Article 73b shall be without prejudice to the right of Member States:

(a) to apply the relevant provisions of their tax law which distinguish between tax-payers who are not in the same situation with regard to their place of residence or with regard to the place where their capital is invested;

(b) to take all requisite measures to prevent infringements of national law and regulations, in particular in the field of taxation and the prudential supervision of financial institutions, or to lay down procedures for the declaration of capital movements for purposes of administrative or statistical information, or to take measures which are justified on grounds of public policy or public security.

2. The provisions of this Chapter shall be without prejudice to the applicability of restrictions on the right of establishment which are compatible with this Treaty.

3. The measures and procedures referred to in paragraphs 1 and 2 shall not constitute a means of arbitrary discrimination or a disguised restriction on the free movement of capital and payments as defined in Article 73b.

Article 73e

By way of derogation from Article 73b, Member States which, on 31 December 1993, enjoy a derogation on the basis of existing Community law, shall be entitled to maintain, until 31 December 1995 at the latest, restrictions on movements of capital authorized by such derogations as exist on that date.

Article 73f

Where, in exceptional circumstances, movements of capital to or from third countries cause, or threaten to cause, serious difficulties for the operation of economic and monetary union, the Council, acting by a qualified majority on a proposal from the Commission and after consulting the ECB, may take safeguard measures with regard to third countries for a period not exceeding six months if such measures are strictly necessary.

Article 73g

1. If, in the cases envisaged in Article 228a, action by the Community is deemed necessary, the Council may, in accordance with the procedure provided for in Article 228a, take the necessary urgent measures on the movement of capital and on payments as regards the third countries concerned.

2. Without prejudice to Article 224 and as long as the Council has not taken measures pursuant to paragraph 1, a Member State may, for serious political reasons and on grounds of urgency, take unilateral measures against a third country with regard to capital movements and payments. The Commission and the other Member States shall be informed of such measures by the date of their entry into force at the latest.

The Council may, acting by a qualified majority on a proposal from the Commission, decide that the Member State concerned shall amend or abolish such measures. The President of the Council shall inform the European Parliament of any such decision taken by the Council.

Article 73h

Until 1 January 1994, the following provisions shall be applicable:

(1) Each Member State undertakes to authorize, in the currency of the Member State in which the creditor or the beneficiary resides, any payments connected with the movement of goods, services or capital, and any transfers of capital and earnings, to the extent that the movement of goods, services, capital and persons between Member States has been liberalized pursuant to this Treaty.

The Member States declare their readiness to undertake the liberalization of payments beyond the extent provided in the preceding subparagraph, in so far as their economic situation in general and the state of their balance of payments in particular so permit.

(2) In so far as movements of goods, services and capital are limited only by restrictions on payments connected therewith, these restrictions shall be progressively abolished by applying, mutatis mutandis, *the provisions of this Chapter and the Chapters relating to the abolition of quantitative restrictions and to the liberalization of services.*

(3) Member States undertake not to introduce between themselves any new restrictions on transfers connected with the invisible transactions listed in Annex III to this Treaty.

The progressive abolition of existing restrictions shall be effected in accordance with the provisions of Articles 63 to 65, in so far as such abolition is not governed by the provisions contained in paragraphs 1 and 2 or by the other provisions of this Chapter.

(4) If need be, Member States shall consult each other on the measures to be taken to enable the payments and transfers mentioned in this Article to be effected; such measures shall not prejudice the attainment of the objectives set out in this Treaty.'

(16) Article 75 shall be replaced by the following:

'Article 75

1. For the purpose of implementing Article 74, and taking into account the distinctive features of transport, the Council shall, acting in accordance with the procedure referred to in Article 189c and after consulting the Economic and Social Committee, lay down:

(a) common rules applicable to international transport to or from the territory of a Member State or passing across the territory of one or more Member States;

(b) the conditions under which non-resident carriers may operate transport services within a Member State;

(c) measures to improve transport safety;

(d) any other appropriate provisions.

2. The provisions referred to in (a) and (b) of paragraph 1 shall be laid down during the transitional period.

3. By way of derogation from the procedure provided for in paragraph 1, where the application of provisions concerning the principles of the regulatory system for transport would be liable to have a serious effect on the standard of living and on employment in certain areas and on the operation of transport facilities, they shall be laid down by the Council acting unanimously on a proposal from the Commission, after consulting the European Parliament and the Economic and Social Committee. In so doing, the Council shall take into account the need for adaptation to the economic development which will result from establishing the common market.'

(17) The title of Title I in Part Three shall be replaced by the following:

'TITLE V

COMMON RULES ON COMPETITION, TAXATION
AND APPROXIMATION OF LAWS'

(18) In Article 92(3):

— the following point shall be inserted:

'(d) aid to promote culture and heritage conservation where such aid does not affect trading conditions and competition in the Community to an extent that is contrary to the common interest.'

— the present point (d) shall become (e).

(19) Article 94 shall be replaced by the following:

'Article 94

The Council, acting by a qualified majority on a proposal from the Commission and after consulting the European Parliament, may make any appropriate regulations for the application of Articles 92 and 93 and may in particular determine the conditions in which Article 93(3) shall apply and the categories of aid exempted from this procedure.'

(20) Article 99 shall be replaced by the following:

'Article 99

The Council shall, acting unanimously on a proposal from the Commission and after consulting the European Parliament and the Economic and Social Committee, adopt provisions for the harmonization of legislation concerning turnover taxes, excise duties and other forms of indirect taxation to the extent that such harmonization is necessary to ensure the establishment and the functioning of the internal market within the time-limit laid down in Article 7a.'

(21) Article 100 shall be replaced by the following:

'Article 100

The Council shall, acting unanimously on a proposal from the Commission and after consulting the European Parliament and the Economic and Social Committee, issue directives for the approximation of such laws, regulations or administrative provisions of the Member States as directly affect the establishment or functioning of the common market.'

(22) Article 100a(1) shall be replaced by the following:

'1. By way of derogation from Article 100 and save where otherwise provided in this Treaty, the following provisions shall apply for the achievement of the objectives set out in Article 7a. The Council shall, acting in accordance with the procedure referred to in Article 189b and after consulting the Economic and Social Committee, adopt the measures for the approximation of the provisions laid down by law, regulation or administrative action in Member States which have as their object the establishment and functioning of the internal market.'

(23) The following Article shall be inserted:

'Article 100c

1. The Council, acting unanimously on a proposal from the Commission and after consulting the European Parliament, shall determine the third countries whose nationals must be in possession of a visa when crossing the external borders of the Member States.

2. However, in the event of an emergency situation in a third country posing a threat of a sudden inflow of nationals from that country into the Community, the Council, acting by a qualified majority on a recommendation from the Commission, may introduce, for a period not exceeding six months, a visa requirement for nationals from the country in question. The visa requirement established under this paragraph may be extended in accordance with the procedure referred to in paragraph 1.

3. From 1 January 1996, the Council shall adopt the decisions referred to in paragraph 1 by a qualified majority. The Council shall, before that date, acting by a qualified majority on a proposal from the Commission and after consulting the European Parliament, adopt measures relating to a uniform format for visas.

4. In the areas referred to in this Article, the Commission shall examine any request made by a Member State that it submit a proposal to the Council.

5. This Article shall be without prejudice to the exercise of the responsibilities incumbent upon the Member States with regard to the maintenance of law and order and the safeguarding of internal security.

6. This Article shall apply to other areas if so decided pursuant to Article K.9 of the provisions of the Treaty on European Union which relate to cooperation in the fields of justice and home affairs, subject to the voting conditions determined at the same time.

7. The provisions of the conventions in force between the Member States governing areas covered by this Article shall remain in force until their content has been replaced by directives or measures adopted pursuant to this Article.'

(24) The following Article shall be inserted:

'Article 100d

The Coordinating Committee consisting of senior officials set up by Article K.4 of the Treaty on European Union shall contribute, without prejudice to the provisions of Article 151, to the preparation of the proceedings of the Council in the fields referred to in Article 100c.'

(25) Title II, Chapters 1, 2 and 3 in Part Three shall be replaced by the following:

'TITLE VI

ECONOMIC AND MONETARY POLICY

CHAPTER 1

Economic policy

Article 102a

Member States shall conduct their economic policies with a view to contributing to the achievement of the objectives of the Community, as defined in Article 2, and in the context of the broad guidelines referred to in Article 103(2). The Member States and the Community shall act in accordance with the principle of an open market economy with free competition, favouring an efficient allocation of resources, and in compliance with the principles set out in Article 3a.

Article 103

1. Member States shall regard their economic policies as a matter of common concern and shall coordinate them within the Council, in accordance with the provisions of Article 102a.

2. The Council shall, acting by a qualified majority on a recommendation from the Commission, formulate a draft for the broad guidelines of the economic policies of the Member States and of the Community, and shall report its findings to the European Council.

The European Council shall, acting on the basis of the report from the Council, discuss a conclusion on the broad guidelines of the economic policies of the Member States and of the Community.

On the basis of this conclusion, the Council shall, acting by a qualified majority, adopt a recommendation setting out these broad guidelines. The Council shall inform the European Parliament of its recommendation.

3. In order to ensure closer coordination of economic policies and sustained convergence of the economic performances of the Member States, the Council shall, on the basis of reports submitted by the Commission, monitor economic developments in each of the Member States and in the Community as well as the consistency of economic policies with the broad guidelines referred to in paragraph 2, and regularly carry out an overall assessment.

For the purpose of this multilateral surveillance, Member States shall forward information to the Commission about important measures taken by them in the field of their economic policy and such other information as they deem necessary.

4. Where it is established, under the procedure referred to in paragraph 3, that the economic policies of a Member State are not consistent with the broad guidelines referred to in paragraph 2 or that they risk jeopardizing the proper functioning of economic and monetary union, the Council may, acting by a qualified majority on a recommendation from the Commission, make the necessary recommendations to the Member State concerned. The Council may, acting by a qualified majority on a proposal from the Commission, decide to make its recommendations public.

The President of the Council and the Commission shall report to the European Parliament on the results of multilateral surveillance. The President of the Council may be invited to appear before the competent Committee of the European Parliament if the Council has made its recommendations public.

5. The Council, acting in accordance with the procedure referred to in Article 189c, may adopt detailed rules for the multilateral surveillance procedure referred to in paragraphs 3 and 4 of this Article.

Article 103a

1. Without prejudice to any other procedures provided for in this Treaty, the Council may, acting unanimously on a proposal from the Commission, decide upon the measures appropriate to the economic situation, in particular if severe difficulties arise in the supply of certain products.

2. Where a Member State is in difficulties or is seriously threatened with severe difficulties caused by exceptional occurrences beyond its control, the Council may, acting unanimously on a proposal from the Commission, grant, under certain conditions, Community financial assistance to the Member State concerned. Where the severe difficulties are caused by natural disasters, the Council shall act by qualified majority. The President of the Council shall inform the European Parliament of the decision taken.

Article 104

1. Overdraft facilities or any other type of credit facility with the ECB or with the central banks of the Member States (hereinafter referred to as "national central banks") in favour of Community institutions or bodies, central governments, regional, local or other public authorities, other bodies governed by public law, or public undertakings of Member States shall be prohibited, as shall the purchase directly from them by the ECB or national central banks of debt instruments.

2. Paragraph 1 shall not apply to publicly owned credit institutions which, in the context of the supply of reserves by central banks, shall be given the same treatment by national central banks and the ECB as private credit institutions.

Article 104a

1. Any measure, not based on prudential considerations, establishing privileged access by Community institutions or bodies, central governments, regional, local or other public authorities, other bodies governed by public law, or public undertakings of Member States to financial institutions shall be prohibited.

2. The Council, acting in accordance with the procedure referred to in Article 189c, shall, before 1 January 1994, specify definitions for the application of the prohibition referred to in paragraph 1.

Article 104b

1. The Community shall not be liable for or assume the commitments of central governments, regional, local or other public authorities, other bodies governed by public law, or public undertakings of any Member State, without prejudice to mutual financial guarantees for the joint execution of a specific project. A Member State shall not be liable for or assume the commitments of central governments, regional, local or other public authorities, other bodies governed by public law or public undertakings of another Member State, without prejudice to mutual financial guarantees for the joint execution of a specific project.

2. If necessary, the Council, acting in accordance with the procedure referred to in Article 189c, may specify definitions for the application of the prohibitions referred to in Article 104 and in this Article.

Article 104c

1. Member States shall avoid excessive government deficits.

2. The Commission shall monitor the development of the budgetary situation and of the stock of government debt in the Member States with a view to identifying gross errors. In particular it shall examine compliance with budgetary discipline on the basis of the following two criteria:

(a) whether the ratio of the planned or actual government deficit to gross domestic product exceeds a reference value, unless

— either the ratio has declined substantially and continuously and reached a level that comes close to the reference value;

— or, alternatively, the excess over the reference value is only exceptional and temporary and the ratio remains close to the reference value;

(b) whether the ratio of government debt to gross domestic product exceeds a reference value, unless the ratio is sufficiently diminishing and approaching the reference value at a satisfactory pace.

The reference values are specified in the Protocol on the excessive deficit procedure annexed to this Treaty.

3. If a Member State does not fulfil the requirements under one or both of these criteria, the Commission shall prepare a report. The report of the Commission shall also take into account whether the government deficit exceeds government investment expenditure and take into account all other relevant factors, including the medium-term economic and budgetary position of the Member State.

The Commission may also prepare a report if, notwithstanding the fulfilment of the requirements under the criteria, it is of the opinion that there is a risk of an excessive deficit in a Member State.

4. The Committee provided for in Article 109c shall formulate an opinion on the report of the Commission.

5. If the Commission considers that an excessive deficit in a Member State exists or may occur, the Commission shall address an opinion to the Council.

6. The Council shall, acting by a qualified majority on a recommendation from the Commission, and having considered any observations which the Member State concerned may wish to make, decide after an overall assessment whether an excessive deficit exists.

7. Where the existence of an excessive deficit is decided according to paragraph 6, the Council shall make recommendations to the Member State concerned with a view to bringing that situation to an end within a given period. Subject to the provisions of paragraph 8, these recommendations shall not be made public.

8. Where it establishes that there has been no effective action in response to its recommendations within the period laid down, the Council may make its recommendations public.

9. If a Member State persists in failing to put into practice the recommendations of the Council, the Council may decide to give notice to the Member State to take, within a specified time-limit, measures for the deficit reduction which is judged necessary by the Council in order to remedy the situation.

In such a case, the Council may request the Member State concerned to submit reports in accordance with a specific timetable in order to examine the adjustment efforts of that Member State.

10. The rights to bring actions provided for in Articles 169 and 170 may not be exercised within the framework of paragraphs 1 to 9 of this Article.

11. As long as a Member State fails to comply with a decision taken in accordance with paragraph 9, the Council may decide to apply or, as the case may be, intensify one or more of the following measures:

— to require the Member State concerned to publish additional information, to be specified by the Council, before issuing bonds and securities;

— to invite the European Investment Bank to reconsider its lending policy towards the Member State concerned;

— to require the Member State concerned to make a non-interest-bearing deposit of an appropriate size with the Community until the excessive deficit has, in the view of the Council, been corrected;

— *to impose fines of an appropriate size.*

The President of the Council shall inform the European Parliament of the decisions taken.

12. *The Council shall abrogate some or all of its decisions referred to in paragraphs 6 to 9 and 11 to the extent that the excessive deficit in the Member State concerned has, in the view of the Council, been corrected. If the Council has previously made public recommendations, it shall, as soon as the decision under paragraph 8 has been abrogated, make a public statement that an excessive deficit in the Member State concerned no longer exists.*

13. *When taking the decisions referred to in paragraphs 7 to 9, 11 and 12, the Council shall act on a recommendation from the Commission by a majority of two-thirds of the votes of its members weighted in accordance with Article 148(2), excluding the votes of the representative of the Member State concerned.*

14. *Further provisions relating to the implementation of the procedure described in this Article are set out in the Protocol on the excessive deficit procedure annexed to this Treaty.*

The Council shall, acting unanimously on a proposal from the Commission and after consulting the European Parliament and the ECB, adopt the appropriate provisions which shall then replace the said Protocol.

Subject to the other provisions of this paragraph the Council shall, before 1 January 1994, acting by a qualified majority on a proposal from the Commission and after consulting the European Parliament, lay down detailed rules and definitions for the application of the provisions of the said Protocol.

CHAPTER 2

Monetary policy

Article 105

1. *The primary objective of the ESCB shall be to maintain price stability. Without prejudice to the objective of price stability, the ESCB shall support the general economic policies in the Community with a view to contributing to the achievement of the objectives of the Community as laid down in Article 2. The ESCB shall act in accordance with the principle of an open market economy with free competition, favouring an efficient allocation of resources, and in compliance with the principles set out in Article 3a.*

2. *The basic tasks to be carried out through the ESCB shall be:*

— *to define and implement the monetary policy of the Community;*

— to conduct foreign-exchange operations consistent with the provisions of Article 109;

— to hold and manage the official foreign reserves of the Member States;

— to promote the smooth operation of payment systems.

3. The third indent of paragraph 2 shall be without prejudice to the holding and management by the governments of Member States of foreign-exchange working balances.

4. The ECB shall be consulted:

— on any proposed Community act in its fields of competence;

— by national authorities regarding any draft legislative provision in its fields of competence, but within the limits and under the conditions set out by the Council in accordance with the procedure laid down in Article 106(6).

The ECB may submit opinions to the appropriate Community institutions or bodies or to national authorities on matters in its fields of competence.

5. The ESCB shall contribute to the smooth conduct of policies pursued by the competent authorities relating to the prudential supervision of credit institutions and the stability of the financial system.

6. The Council may, acting unanimously on a proposal from the Commission and after consulting the ECB and after receiving the assent of the European Parliament, confer upon the ECB specific tasks concerning policies relating to the prudential supervision of credit institutions and other financial institutions with the exception of insurance undertakings.

Article 105a

1. The ECB shall have the exclusive right to authorize the issue of banknotes within the Community. The ECB and the national central banks may issue such notes. The banknotes issued by the ECB and the national central banks shall be the only such notes to have the status of legal tender within the Community.

2. Member States may issue coins subject to approval by the ECB of the volume of the issue. The Council may, acting in accordance with the procedure referred to in Article 189c and after consulting the ECB, adopt measures to harmonize the denominations and technical specifications of all coins intended for circulation to the extent necessary to permit their smooth circulation within the Community.

Article 106

1. The ESCB shall be composed of the ECB and of the national central banks.

2. The ECB shall have legal personality.

3. The ESCB shall be governed by the decision-making bodies of the ECB which shall be the Governing Council and the Executive Board.

4. The Statute of the ESCB is laid down in a Protocol annexed to this Treaty.

5. Articles 5.1, 5.2, 5.3, 17, 18, 19.1, 22, 23, 24, 26, 32.2, 32.3, 32.4, 32.6, 33.1(a) and 36 of the Statute of the ESCB may be amended by the Council, acting either by a qualified majority on a recommendation from the ECB and after consulting the Commission or unanimously on a proposal from the Commission and after consulting the ECB. In either case, the assent of the European Parliament shall be required.

6. The Council, acting by a qualified majority either on a proposal from the Commission and after consulting the European Parliament and the ECB or on a recommendation from the ECB and after consulting the European Parliament and the Commission, shall adopt the provisions referred to in Articles 4, 5.4, 19.2, 20, 28.1, 29.2, 30.4 and 34.3 of the Statute of the ESCB.

Article 107

When exercising the powers and carrying out the tasks and duties conferred upon them by this Treaty and the Statute of the ESCB, neither the ECB, nor a national central bank, nor any member of their decision-making bodies shall seek or take instructions from Community institutions or bodies, from any government of a Member State or from any other body. The Community institutions and bodies and the governments of the Member States undertake to respect this principle and not to seek to influence the members of the decision-making bodies of the ECB or of the national central banks in the performance of their tasks.

Article 108

Each Member State shall ensure, at the latest at the date of the establishment of the ESCB, that its national legislation including the statutes of its national central bank is compatible with this Treaty and the Statute of the ESCB.

Article 108a

1. In order to carry out the tasks entrusted to the ESCB, the ECB shall, in accordance with the provisions of this Treaty and under the conditions laid down in the Statute of the ESCB:

— *make regulations to the extent necessary to implement the tasks defined in Article 3.1, first indent, Articles 19.1, 22 and 25.2 of the Statute of the ESCB and in cases which shall be laid down in the acts of the Council referred to in Article 106(6);*

— *take decisions necessary for carrying out the tasks entrusted to the ESCB under this Treaty and the Statute of the ESCB;*

— *make recommendations and deliver opinions.*

2. A regulation shall have general application. It shall be binding in its entirety and directly applicable in all Member States.

Recommendations and opinions shall have no binding force.

A decision shall be binding in its entirety upon those to whom it is addressed.

Articles 190 to 192 shall apply to regulations and decisions adopted by the ECB.

The ECB may decide to publish its decisions, recommendations and opinions.

3. Within the limits and under the conditions adopted by the Council under the procedure laid down in Article 106(6), the ECB shall be entitled to impose fines or periodic penalty payments on undertakings for failure to comply with obligations under its regulations and decisions.

Article 109

1. By way of derogation from Article 228, the Council may, acting unanimously on a recommendation from the ECB or from the Commission, and after consulting the ECB in an endeavour to reach a consensus consistent with the objective of price stability, after consulting the European Parliament, in accordance with the procedure in paragraph 3 for determining the arrangements, conclude formal agreements on an exchange-rate system for the ecu in relation to non-Community currencies. The Council may, acting by a qualified majority on a recommendation from the ECB or from the Commission, and after consulting the ECB in an endeavour to reach a consensus consistent with the objective of price stability, adopt, adjust or abandon the central rates of the ecu within the exchange-rate system. The President of the Council shall inform the European Parliament of the adoption, adjustment or abandonment of the ecu central rates.

2. In the absence of an exchange-rate system in relation to one or more non-Community currencies as referred to in paragraph 1, the Council, acting by a qualified majority either on a recommendation from the Commission and after consulting the ECB or on a recommendation from the ECB, may formulate general orientations for exchange-rate policy in relation to these currencies. These general orientations shall be without prejudice to the primary objective of the ESCB to maintain price stability.

3. By way of derogation from Article 228, where agreements concerning monetary or foreign-exchange regime matters need to be negotiated by the Community with one or more States or international organizations, the Council, acting by a qualified majority on a recommendation from the Commission and after consulting the ECB, shall decide the arrangements for the negotiation and for the conclusion of such agreements. These arrangements shall ensure that the Community expresses a single position. The Commission shall be fully associated with the negotiations.

Agreements concluded in accordance with this paragraph shall be binding on the institutions of the Community, on the ECB and on Member States.

4. Subject to paragraph 1, the Council shall, on a proposal from the Commission and after consulting the ECB, acting by a qualified majority decide on the position of the Community at international level as regards issues of particular relevance to economic and monetary union and, acting unanimously, decide its representation in compliance with the allocation of powers laid down in Articles 103 and 105.

5. Without prejudice to Community competence and Community agreements as regards economic and monetary union, Member States may negotiate in international bodies and conclude international agreements.

CHAPTER 3

Institutional provisions

Article 109a

1. The Governing Council of the ECB shall comprise the members of the Executive Board of the ECB and the Governors of the national central banks.

2. (a) The Executive Board shall comprise the President, the Vice-President and four other members.

   (b) The President, the Vice-President and the other members of the Executive Board shall be appointed from among persons of recognized standing and professional experience in monetary or banking matters by common accord of the governments of the Member States at the level of Heads of State or Government, on a recommendation from the Council, after it has consulted the European Parliament and the Governing Council of the ECB.

Their term of office shall be eight years and shall not be renewable.

Only nationals of Member States may be members of the Executive Board.

Article 109b

1. The President of the Council and a member of the Commission may participate, without having the right to vote, in meetings of the Governing Council of the ECB.

The President of the Council may submit a motion for deliberation to the Governing Council of the ECB.

2. The President of the ECB shall be invited to participate in Council meetings when the Council is discussing matters relating to the objectives and tasks of the ESCB.

3. The ECB shall address an annual report on the activities of the ESCB and on the monetary policy of both the previous and current year to the European Parliament, the Council and the Commission, and also to the European Council. The President of the ECB shall present this report to the Council and to the European Parliament, which may hold a general debate on that basis.

The President of the ECB and the other members of the Executive Board may, at the request of the European Parliament or on their own initiative, be heard by the competent Committees of the European Parliament.

Article 109c

1. In order to promote coordination of the policies of Member States to the full extent needed for the functioning of the internal market, a Monetary Committee with advisory status is hereby set up.

It shall have the following tasks:

— *to keep under review the monetary and financial situation of the Member States and of the Community and the general payments system of the Member States and to report regularly thereon to the Council and to the Commission;*

— *to deliver opinions at the request of the Council or of the Commission, or on its own initiative for submission to those institutions;*

— *without prejudice to Article 151, to contribute to the preparation of the work of the Council referred to in Articles 73f, 73g, 103(2), (3), (4) and (5), 103a, 104a, 104b, 104c, 109e(2), 109f(6), 109h, 109i, 109j(2) and 109k(1);*

— to examine, at least once a year, the situation regarding the movement of capital and the freedom of payments, as they result from the application of this Treaty and of measures adopted by the Council; the examination shall cover all measures relating to capital movements and payments; the Committee shall report to the Commission and to the Council on the outcome of this examination.

The Member States and the Commission shall each appoint two members of the Monetary Committee.

2. At the start of the third stage, an Economic and Financial Committee shall be set up. The Monetary Committee provided for in paragraph 1 shall be dissolved.

The Economic and Financial Committee shall have the following tasks:

— to deliver opinions at the request of the Council or of the Commission, or on its own initiative for submission to those institutions;

— to keep under review the economic and financial situation of the Member States and of the Community and to report regularly thereon to the Council and to the Commission, in particular on financial relations with third countries and international institutions;

— without prejudice to Article 151, to contribute to the preparation of the work of the Council referred to in Articles 73f, 73g, 103(2), (3), (4) and (5), 103a, 104a, 104b, 104c, 105(6), 105a(2), 106(5) and (6), 109, 109h, 109i(2) and (3), 109k(2), 109l(4) and (5), and to carry out other advisory and preparatory tasks assigned to it by the Council;

— to examine, at least once a year, the situation regarding the movement of capital and the freedom of payments, as they result from the application of this Treaty and of measures adopted by the Council; the examination shall cover all measures relating to capital movements and payments; the Committee shall report to the Commission and to the Council on the outcome of this examination.

The Member States, the Commission and the ECB shall each appoint no more than two members of the Committee.

3. The Council shall, acting by a qualified majority on a proposal from the Commission and after consulting the ECB and the Committee referred to in this Article, lay down detailed provisions concerning the composition of the Economic and Financial Committee. The President of the Council shall inform the European Parliament of such a decision.

4. In addition to the tasks set out in paragraph 2, if and as long as there are Member States with a derogation as referred to in Articles 109k and 109l, the Committee shall keep under review the monetary and financial situation and the

general payments system of those Member States and report regularly thereon to the Council and to the Commission.

Article 109d

For matters within the scope of Articles 103(4), 104c with the exception of paragraph 14, 109, 109j, 109k and 109l(4) and (5), the Council or a Member State may request the Commission to make a recommendation or a proposal, as appropriate. The Commission shall examine this request and submit its conclusions to the Council without delay.

CHAPTER 4

Transitional provisions

Article 109e

1. The second stage for achieving economic and monetary union shall begin on 1 January 1994.

2. Before that date

(a) each Member State shall:

— adopt, where necessary, appropriate measures to comply with the prohibitions laid down in Article 73b, without prejudice to Article 73e, and in Articles 104 and 104a(1);

— adopt, if necessary, with a view to permitting the assessment provided for in subparagraph (b), multiannual programmes intended to ensure the lasting convergence necessary for the achievement of economic and monetary union, in particular with regard to price stability and sound public finances;

(b) the Council shall, on the basis of a report from the Commission, assess the progress made with regard to economic and monetary convergence, in particular with regard to price stability and sound public finances, and the progress made with the implementation of Community law concerning the internal market.

3. The provisions of Articles 104, 104a(1), 104b(1) and 104c with the exception of paragraphs 1, 9, 11 and 14 shall apply from the beginning of the second stage.

The provisions of Articles 103a(2), 104c(1), (9) and (11), 105, 105a, 107, 109, 109a, 109b and 109c(2) and (4) shall apply from the beginning of the third stage.

4. In the second stage, Member States shall endeavour to avoid excessive government deficits.

5. During the second stage, each Member State shall, as appropriate, start the process leading to the independence of its central bank, in accordance with Article 108.

Article 109f

1. At the start of the second stage, a European Monetary Institute (hereinafter referred to as "EMI") shall be established and take up its duties; it shall have legal personality and be directed and managed by a Council, consisting of a President and the Governors of the national central banks, one of whom shall be Vice-President.

The President shall be appointed by common accord of the governments of the Member States at the level of Heads of State or Government, on a recommendation from, as the case may be, the Committee of Governors of the central banks of the Member States (hereinafter referred to as "Committee of Governors") or the Council of the EMI, and after consulting the European Parliament and the Council. The President shall be selected from among persons of recognized standing and professional experience in monetary or banking matters. Only nationals of Member States may be President of the EMI. The Council of the EMI shall appoint the Vice-President.

The Statute of the EMI is laid down in a Protocol annexed to this Treaty.

The Committee of Governors shall be dissolved at the start of the second stage.

2. The EMI shall:

— strengthen cooperation between the national central banks;

— strengthen the coordination of the monetary policies of the Member States, with the aim of ensuring price stability;

— monitor the functioning of the European Monetary System;

— hold consultations concerning issues falling within the competence of the national central banks and affecting the stability of financial institutions and markets;

— take over the tasks of the European Monetary Cooperation Fund, which shall be dissolved; the modalities of dissolution are laid down in the Statute of the EMI;

— *facilitate the use of the ecu and oversee its development, including the smooth functioning of the ecu clearing system.*

3. For the preparation of the third stage, the EMI shall:

— *prepare the instruments and the procedures necessary for carrying out a single monetary policy in the third stage;*

— *promote the harmonization, where necessary, of the rules and practices governing the collection, compilation and distribution of statistics in the areas within its field of competence;*

— *prepare the rules for operations to be undertaken by the national central banks within the framework of the ESCB;*

— *promote the efficiency of cross-border payments;*

— *supervise the technical preparation of ecu banknotes.*

At the latest by 31 December 1996, the EMI shall specify the regulatory, organizational and logistical framework necessary for the ESCB to perform its tasks in the third stage. This framework shall be submitted for decision to the ECB at the date of its establishment.

4. The EMI, acting by a majority of two-thirds of the members of its Council, may:

— *formulate opinions or recommendations on the overall orientation of monetary policy and exchange-rate policy as well as on related measures introduced in each Member State;*

— *submit opinions or recommendations to governments and to the Council on policies which might affect the internal or external monetary situation in the Community and, in particular, the functioning of the European Monetary System;*

— *make recommendations to the monetary authorities of the Member States concerning the conduct of their monetary policy.*

5. The EMI, acting unanimously, may decide to publish its opinions and its recommendations.

6. The EMI shall be consulted by the Council regarding any proposed Community act within its field of competence.

Within the limits and under the conditions set out by the Council, acting by a qualified majority on a proposal from the Commission and after consulting the European Parliament and the EMI, the EMI shall be consulted by the authorities of the Member States on any draft legislative provision within its field of competence.

7. *The Council may, acting unanimously on a proposal from the Commission and after consulting the European Parliament and the EMI, confer upon the EMI other tasks for the preparation of the third stage.*

8. *Where this Treaty provides for a consultative role for the ECB, references to the ECB shall be read as referring to the EMI before the establishment of the ECB.*

Where this Treaty provides for a consultative role for the EMI, references to the EMI shall be read, before 1 January 1994, as referring to the Committee of Governors.

9. *During the second stage, the term "ECB" used in Articles 173, 175, 176, 177, 180 and 215 shall be read as referring to the EMI.*

Article 109g

The currency composition of the ecu basket shall not be changed.

From the start of the third stage, the value of the ecu shall be irrevocably fixed in accordance with Article 109l(4).

Article 109h

1. *Where a Member State is in difficulties or is seriously threatened with difficulties as regards its balance of payments either as a result of an overall disequilibrium in its balance of payments, or as a result of the type of currency at its disposal, and where such difficulties are liable in particular to jeopardize the functioning of the common market or the progressive implementation of the common commercial policy, the Commission shall immediately investigate the position of the State in question and the action which, making use of all the means at its disposal, that State has taken or may take in accordance with the provisions of this Treaty. The Commission shall state what measures it recommends the State concerned to take.*

If the action taken by a Member State and the measures suggested by the Commission do not prove sufficient to overcome the difficulties which have arisen or which threaten, the Commission shall, after consulting the Committee referred to in Article 109c, recommend to the Council the granting of mutual assistance and appropriate methods therefor.

The Commission shall keep the Council regularly informed of the situation and of how it is developing.

2. *The Council, acting by a qualified majority, shall grant such mutual assistance; it shall adopt directives or decisions laying down the conditions and details of such assistance, which may take such forms as:*

(a) a concerted approach to or within any other international organizations to which Member States may have recourse;

(b) *measures needed to avoid deflection of trade where the State which is in difficulties maintains or reintroduces quantitative restrictions against third countries;*

(c) *the granting of limited credits by other Member States, subject to their agreement.*

3. *If the mutual assistance recommended by the Commission is not granted by the Council or if the mutual assistance granted and the measures taken are insufficient, the Commission shall authorize the State which is in difficulties to take protective measures, the conditions and details of which the Commission shall determine.*

Such authorization may be revoked and such conditions and details may be changed by the Council acting by a qualified majority.

4. *Subject to Article 109k(6), this Article shall cease to apply from the beginning of the third stage.*

Article 109i

1. *Where a sudden crisis in the balance of payments occurs and a decision within the meaning of Article 109h(2) is not immediately taken, the Member State concerned may, as a precaution, take the necessary protective measures. Such measures must cause the least possible disturbance in the functioning of the common market and must not be wider in scope than is strictly necessary to remedy the sudden difficulties which have arisen.*

2. *The Commission and the other Member States shall be informed of such protective measures not later than when they enter into force. The Commission may recommend to the Council the granting of mutual assistance under Article 109h.*

3. *After the Commission has delivered an opinion and the Committee referred to in Article 109c has been consulted, the Council may, acting by a qualified majority, decide that the State concerned shall amend, suspend or abolish the protective measures referred to above.*

4. *Subject to Article 109k(6), this Article shall cease to apply from the beginning of the third stage.*

Article 109j

1. *The Commission and the EMI shall report to the Council on the progress made in the fulfilment by the Member States of their obligations regarding the achievement of economic and monetary union. These reports shall include an examination of the compatibility between each Member State's national legislation, including the statutes of its national central bank, and Articles 107 and*

108 of this Treaty and the Statute of the ESCB. The reports shall also examine the achievement of a high degree of sustainable convergence by reference to the fulfilment by each Member State of the following criteria:

— *the achievement of a high degree of price stability; this will be apparent from a rate of inflation which is close to that of, at most, the three best performing Member States in terms of price stability;*

— *the sustainability of the government financial position; this will be apparent from having achieved a government budgetary position without a deficit that is excessive as determined in accordance with Article 104c(6);*

— *the observance of the normal fluctuation margins provided for by the exchange-rate mechanism of the European Monetary System, for at least two years, without devaluing against the currency of any other Member State;*

— *the durability of convergence achieved by the Member State and of its participation in the exchange-rate mechanism of the European Monetary System being reflected in the long-term interest-rate levels.*

The four criteria mentioned in this paragraph and the relevant periods over which they are to be respected are developed further in a Protocol annexed to this Treaty. The reports of the Commission and the EMI shall also take account of the development of the ecu, the results of the integration of markets, the situation and development of the balances of payments on current account and an examination of the development of unit labour costs and other price indices.

2. On the basis of these reports, the Council, acting by a qualified majority on a recommendation from the Commission, shall assess:

— *for each Member State, whether it fulfils the necessary conditions for the adoption of a single currency;*

— *whether a majority of the Member States fulfil the necessary conditions for the adoption of a single currency,*

and recommend its findings to the Council, meeting in the composition of the Heads of State or Government. The European Parliament shall be consulted and forward its opinion to the Council, meeting in the composition of the Heads of State or Government.

3. Taking due account of the reports referred to in paragraph 1 and the opinion of the European Parliament referred to in paragraph 2, the Council, meeting in the composition of Heads of State or Government, shall, acting by a qualified majority, not later than 31 December 1996:

— *decide, on the basis of the recommendations of the Council referred to in paragraph 2, whether a majority of the Member States fulfil the necessary conditions for the adoption of a single currency;*

— *decide whether it is appropriate for the Community to enter the third stage,*

and if so

— *set the date for the beginning of the third stage.*

4. If by the end of 1997 the date for the beginning of the third stage has not been set, the third stage shall start on 1 January 1999. Before 1 July 1998, the Council, meeting in the composition of Heads of State or Government, after a repetition of the procedure provided for in paragraphs 1 and 2, with the exception of the second indent of paragraph 2, taking into account the reports referred to in paragraph 1 and the opinion of the European Parliament, shall, acting by a qualified majority and on the basis of the recommendations of the Council referred to in paragraph 2, confirm which Member States fulfil the necessary conditions for the adoption of a single currency.

Article 109k

1. If the decision has been taken to set the date in accordance with Article 109j(3), the Council shall, on the basis of its recommendations referred to in Article 109j(2), acting by a qualified majority on a recommendation from the Commission, decide whether any, and if so which, Member States shall have a derogation as defined in paragraph 3 of this Article. Such Member States shall in this Treaty be referred to as "Member States with a derogation".

If the Council has confirmed which Member States fulfil the necessary conditions for the adoption of a single currency, in accordance with Article 109j(4), those Member States which do not fulfil the conditions shall have a derogation as defined in paragraph 3 of this Article. Such Member States shall in this Treaty be referred to as "Member States with a derogation".

2. At least once every two years, or at the request of a Member State with a derogation, the Commission and the ECB shall report to the Council in accordance with the procedure laid down in Article 109j(1). After consulting the European Parliament and after discussion in the Council, meeting in the composition of the Heads of State or Government, the Council shall, acting by a qualified majority on a proposal from the Commission, decide which Member States with a derogation fulfil the necessary conditions on the basis of the criteria set out in Article 109j(1), and abrogate the derogations of the Member States concerned.

3. A derogation referred to in paragraph 1 shall entail that the following Articles do not apply to the Member State concerned: Articles 104c(9) and (11), 105(1), (2), (3) and (5), 105a, 108a, 109, and 109a(2)(b). The exclusion of such a Member State and its national central bank from rights and obligations within the ESCB is laid down in Chapter IX of the Statute of the ESCB.

4. In Articles 105(1), (2) and (3), 105a, 108a, 109 and 109a(2)(b), "Member States" shall be read as "Member States without a derogation".

5. The voting rights of Member States with a derogation shall be suspended for the Council decisions referred to in the Articles of this Treaty mentioned in paragraph 3. In that case, by way of derogation from Articles 148 and 189a(1), a qualified majority shall be defined as two-thirds of the votes of the representatives of the Member States without a derogation weighted in accordance with Article 148(2), and unanimity of those Member States shall be required for an act requiring unanimity.

6. Articles 109h and 109i shall continue to apply to a Member State with a derogation.

Article 109l

1. Immediately after the decision on the date for the beginning of the third stage has been taken in accordance with Article 109j(3), or, as the case may be, immediately after 1 July 1998:

— the Council shall adopt the provisions referred to in Article 106(6);

— the governments of the Member States without a derogation shall appoint, in accordance with the procedure set out in Article 50 of the Statute of the ESCB, the President, the Vice-President and the other members of the Executive Board of the ECB. If there are Member States with a derogation, the number of members of the Executive Board may be smaller than provided for in Article 11.1 of the Statute of the ESCB, but in no circumstances shall it be less than four.

As soon as the Executive Board is appointed, the ESCB and the ECB shall be established and shall prepare for their full operation as described in this Treaty and the Statute of the ESCB. The full exercise of their powers shall start from the first day of the third stage.

2. As soon as the ECB is established, it shall, if necessary, take over tasks of the EMI. The EMI shall go into liquidation upon the establishment of the ECB; the modalities of liquidation are laid down in the Statute of the EMI.

3. If and as long as there are Member States with a derogation, and without prejudice to Article 106(3) of this Treaty, the General Council of the ECB referred to in Article 45 of the Statute of the ESCB shall be constituted as a third decision-making body of the ECB.

4. At the starting date of the third stage, the Council shall, acting with the unanimity of the Member States without a derogation, on a proposal from the Commission and after consulting the ECB, adopt the conversion rates at which their currencies shall be irrevocably fixed and at which irrevocably fixed rate the ecu shall be substituted for these currencies, and the ecu will become a currency

in its own right. *This measure shall by itself not modify the external value of the ecu. The Council shall, acting according to the same procedure, also take the other measures necessary for the rapid introduction of the ecu as the single currency of those Member States.*

5. If it is decided, according to the procedure set out in Article 109k(2), to abrogate a derogation, the Council shall, acting with the unanimity of the Member States without a derogation and the Member State concerned, on a proposal from the Commission and after consulting the ECB, adopt the rate at which the ecu shall be substituted for the currency of the Member State concerned, and take the other measures necessary for the introduction of the ecu as the single currency in the Member State concerned.

Article 109m

1. Until the beginning of the third stage, each Member State shall treat its exchange-rate policy as a matter of common interest. In so doing, Member States shall take account of the experience acquired in cooperation within the framework of the European Monetary System (EMS) and in developing the ecu, and shall respect existing powers in this field.

2. From the beginning of the third stage and for as long as a Member State has a derogation, paragraph 1 shall apply by analogy to the exchange-rate policy of that Member State.'

(26) In Title II of Part Three, the title of Chapter 4 shall be replaced by the following:

'TITLE VII

COMMON COMMERCIAL POLICY'

(27) Article 111 shall be repealed.

(28) Article 113 shall be replaced by the following:

'Article 113

1. The common commercial policy shall be based on uniform principles, particularly in regard to changes in tariff rates, the conclusion of tariff and trade agreements, the achievement of uniformity in measures of liberalization, export policy and measures to protect trade such as those to be taken in the event of dumping or subsidies.

2. The Commission shall submit proposals to the Council for implementing the common commercial policy.

3. Where agreements with one or more States or international organizations need to be negotiated, the Commission shall make recommendations to the Council, which shall authorize the Commission to open the necessary negotiations.

The Commission shall conduct these negotiations in consultation with a special committee appointed by the Council to assist the Commission in this task and within the framework of such directives as the Council may issue to it.

The relevant provisions of Article 228 shall apply.

4. In exercising the powers conferred upon it by this Article, the Council shall act by a qualified majority.'

(29) Article 114 shall be repealed.

(30) Article 115 shall be replaced by the following:

'Article 115

In order to ensure that the execution of measures of commercial policy taken in accordance with this Treaty by any Member State is not obstructed by deflection of trade, or where differences between such measures lead to economic difficulties in one or more Member States, the Commission shall recommend the methods for the requisite cooperation between Member States. Failing this, the Commission may authorize Member States to take the necessary protective measures, the conditions and details of which it shall determine.

In case of urgency, Member States shall request authorization to take the necessary measures themselves from the Commission, which shall take a decision as soon as possible; the Member States concerned shall then notify the measures to the other Member States. The Commission may decide at any time that the Member States concerned shall amend or abolish the measures in question.

In the selection of such measures, priority shall be given to those which cause the least disturbance to the functioning of the common market.'

(31) Article 116 shall be repealed.

(32) In Part Three, the title of Title III shall be replaced by the following:

'TITLE VIII

SOCIAL POLICY, EDUCATION, VOCATIONAL TRAINING AND YOUTH'

(33) The first subparagraph of Article 118a(2) shall be replaced by the following:

'2. In order to help achieve the objective laid down in the first paragraph, the Council, acting in accordance with the procedure referred to in Article 189c and after consulting the Economic and Social Committee, shall adopt by means of directives, minimum requirements for gradual implementation, having regard to the conditions and technical rules obtaining in each of the Member States.'

(34) Article 123 shall be replaced by the following:

'Article 123

In order to improve employment opportunities for workers in the internal market and to contribute thereby to raising the standard of living, a European Social Fund is hereby established in accordance with the provisions set out below; it shall aim to render the employment of workers easier and to increase their geographical and occupational mobility within the Community, and to facilitate their adaptation to industrial changes and to changes in production systems, in particular through vocational training and retraining.'

(35) Article 125 shall be replaced by the following:

'Article 125

The Council, acting in accordance with the procedure referred to in Article 189c and after consulting the Economic and Social Committee, shall adopt implementing decisions relating to the European Social Fund.'

(36) Articles 126, 127 and 128 shall be replaced by the following:

'CHAPTER 3

Education, vocational training and youth

Article 126

1. The Community shall contribute to the development of quality education by encouraging cooperation between Member States and, if necessary, by supporting and supplementing their action, while fully respecting the responsibility of the Member States for the content of teaching and the organization of education systems and their cultural and linguistic diversity.

2. Community action shall be aimed at:

— *developing the European dimension in education, particularly through the teaching and dissemination of the languages of the Member States;*

— *encouraging mobility of students and teachers,* inter alia *by encouraging the academic recognition of diplomas and periods of study;*

— *promoting cooperation between educational establishments;*

— *developing exchanges of information and experience on issues common to the education systems of the Member States;*

— *encouraging the development of youth exchanges and of exchanges of socio-educational instructors;*

— *encouraging the development of distance education.*

3. The Community and the Member States shall foster cooperation with third countries and the competent international organizations in the field of education, in particular the Council of Europe.

4. In order to contribute to the achievement of the objectives referred to in this Article, the Council:

— *acting in accordance with the procedure referred to in Article 189b, after consulting the Economic and Social Committee and the Committee of the Regions, shall adopt incentive measures, excluding any harmonization of the laws and regulations of the Member States;*

— *acting by a qualified majority on a proposal from the Commission, shall adopt recommendations.*

Article 127

1. The Community shall implement a vocational training policy which shall support and supplement the action of the Member States, while fully respecting the responsibility of the Member States for the content and organization of vocational training.

2. Community action shall aim to:

— facilitate adaptation to industrial changes, in particular through vocational training and retraining;

— improve initial and continuing vocational training in order to facilitate vocational integration and reintegration into the labour market;

— facilitate access to vocational training and encourage mobility of instructors and trainees and particularly young people;

— stimulate cooperation on training between educational or training establishments and firms;

— develop exchanges of information and experience on issues common to the training systems of the Member States.

3. The Community and the Member States shall foster cooperation with third countries and the competent international organizations in the sphere of vocational training.

4. The Council, acting in accordance with the procedure referred to in Article 189c and after consulting the Economic and Social Committee, shall adopt measures to contribute to the achievement of the objectives referred to in this Article, excluding any harmonization of the laws and regulations of the Member States.'

(37) The following shall be inserted:

'TITLE IX

CULTURE

Article 128

1. The Community shall contribute to the flowering of the cultures of the Member States, while respecting their national and regional diversity and at the same time bringing the common cultural heritage to the fore.

2. Action by the Community shall be aimed at encouraging cooperation between Member States and, if necessary, supporting and supplementing their action in the following areas:

— *improvement of the knowledge and dissemination of the culture and history of the European peoples;*

— *conservation and safeguarding of cultural heritage of European significance;*

— *non-commercial cultural exchanges;*

— *artistic and literary creation, including in the audiovisual sector.*

3. The Community and the Member States shall foster cooperation with third countries and the competent international organizations in the sphere of culture, in particular the Council of Europe.

4. The Community shall take cultural aspects into account in its action under other provisions of this Treaty.

5. In order to contribute to the achievement of the objectives referred to in this Article, the Council:

— *acting in accordance with the procedure referred to in Article 189b and after consulting the Committee of the Regions, shall adopt incentive measures, excluding any harmonization of the laws and regulations of the Member States. The Council shall act unanimously throughout the procedures referred to in Article 189b;*

— *acting unanimously on a proposal from the Commission, shall adopt recommendations.'*

(38) Titles IV, V, VI and VII shall be replaced by the following:

'*TITLE X*

PUBLIC HEALTH

Article 129

1. The Community shall contribute towards ensuring a high level of human health protection by encouraging cooperation between the Member States and, if necessary, lending support to their action.

Community action shall be directed towards the prevention of diseases, in particular the major health scourges, including drug dependence, by promoting research into their causes and their transmission, as well as health information and education.

Health protection requirements shall form a constituent part of the Community's other policies.

2. Member States shall, in liaison with the Commission, coordinate among themselves their policies and programmes in the areas referred to in paragraph 1. The Commission may, in close contact with the Member States, take any useful initiative to promote such coordination.

3. The Community and the Member States shall foster cooperation with third countries and the competent international organizations in the sphere of public health.

4. In order to contribute to the achievement of the objectives referred to in this Article, the Council:

— *acting in accordance with the procedure referred to in Article 189b, after consulting the Economic and Social Committee and the Committee of the Regions, shall adopt incentive measures, excluding any harmonization of the laws and regulations of the Member States;*

— *acting by a qualified majority on a proposal from the Commission, shall adopt recommendations.*

TITLE XI

CONSUMER PROTECTION

Article 129a

1. The Community shall contribute to the attainment of a high level of consumer protection through:

(a) *measures adopted pursuant to Article 100a in the context of the completion of the internal market;*

(b) *specific action which supports and supplements the policy pursued by the Member States to protect the health, safety and economic interests of consumers and to provide adequate information to consumers.*

2. The Council, acting in accordance with the procedure referred to in Article 189b and after consulting the Economic and Social Committee, shall adopt the specific action referred to in paragraph 1(b).

3. Action adopted pursuant to paragraph 2 shall not prevent any Member State from maintaining or introducing more stringent protective measures. Such measures must be compatible with this Treaty. The Commission shall be notified of them.

TITLE XII

TRANS-EUROPEAN NETWORKS

Article 129b

1. To help achieve the objectives referred to in Articles 7a and 130a and to enable citizens of the Union, economic operators and regional and local communities to derive full benefit from the setting up of an area without internal frontiers, the Community shall contribute to the establishment and development of trans-European networks in the areas of transport, telecommunications and energy infrastructures.

2. Within the framework of a system of open and competitive markets, action by the Community shall aim at promoting the interconnection and interoperability of national networks as well as access to such networks. It shall take account in particular of the need to link island, landlocked and peripheral regions with the central regions of the Community.

Article 129c

1. In order to achieve the objectives referred to in Article 129b, the Community:

— *shall establish a series of guidelines covering the objectives, priorities and broad lines of measures envisaged in the sphere of trans-European networks; these guidelines shall identify projects of common interest;*

— *shall implement any measures that may prove necessary to ensure the interoperability of the networks, in particular in the field of technical standardization;*

— *may support the financial efforts made by the Member States for projects of common interest financed by Member States, which are identified in the framework of the guidelines referred to in the first indent, particularly through feasibility studies, loan guarantees or interest-rate subsidies; the Community may also contribute, through the Cohesion Fund to be set up no later than 31 December 1993 pursuant to Article 130d, to the financing of specific projects in Member States in the area of transport infrastructure.*

The Community's activities shall take into account the potential economic viability of the projects.

2. Member States shall, in liaison with the Commission, coordinate among themselves the policies pursued at national level which may have a significant impact on the achievement of the objectives referred to in Article 129b. The Commission may, in close cooperation with the Member States, take any useful initiative to promote such coordination.

3. The Community may decide to cooperate with third countries to promote projects of mutual interest and to ensure the interoperability of networks.

Article 129d

The guidelines referred to in Article 129c(1) shall be adopted by the Council, acting in accordance with the procedure referred to in Article 189b and after consulting the Economic and Social Committee and the Committee of the Regions.

Guidelines and projects of common interest which relate to the territory of a Member State shall require the approval of the Member State concerned.

The Council, acting in accordance with the procedure referred to in Article 189c and after consulting the Economic and Social Committee and the Committee of the Regions, shall adopt the other measures provided for in Article 129c(1).

TITLE XIII

INDUSTRY

Article 130

1. The Community and the Member States shall ensure that the conditions necessary for the competitiveness of the Community's industry exist.

For that purpose, in accordance with a system of open and competitive markets, their action shall be aimed at:

— *speeding up the adjustment of industry to structural changes;*

— *encouraging an environment favourable to initiative and to the development of undertakings throughout the Community, particularly small and medium-sized undertakings;*

— *encouraging an environment favourable to cooperation between undertakings;*

— *fostering better exploitation of the industrial potential of policies of innovation, research and technological development.*

2. The Member States shall consult each other in liaison with the Commission and, where necessary, shall coordinate their action. The Commission may take any useful initiative to promote such coordination.

3. The Community shall contribute to the achievement of the objectives set out in paragraph 1 through the policies and activities it pursues under other provisions of this Treaty. The Council, acting unanimously on a proposal from the Commission, after consulting the European Parliament and the Economic and Social Committee, may decide on specific measures in support of action taken in the Member States to achieve the objectives set out in paragraph 1.

This Title shall not provide a basis for the introduction by the Community of any measure which could lead to a distortion of competition.

TITLE XIV

ECONOMIC AND SOCIAL COHESION

Article 130a

In order to promote its overall harmonious development, the Community shall develop and pursue its actions leading to the strengthening of its economic and social cohesion.

In particular, the Community shall aim at reducing disparities between the levels of development of the various regions and the backwardness of the least favoured regions, including rural areas.

Article 130b

Member States shall conduct their economic policies and shall coordinate them in such a way as, in addition, to attain the objectives set out in Article 130a. The formulation and implementation of the Community's policies and actions and the implementation of the internal market shall take into account the objectives set out in Article 130a and shall contribute to their achievement. The Community shall also support the achievement of these objectives by the action it takes through the structural Funds (European Agricultural Guidance and Guarantee Fund — Guidance Section; European Social Fund; European Regional Development Fund), the European Investment Bank and the other existing financial instruments.

The Commission shall submit a report to the European Parliament, the Council, the Economic and Social Committee and the Committee of the Regions every three years on the progress made towards achieving economic and social cohesion and on the manner in which the various means provided for in this Article have contributed to it. This report shall, if necessary, be accompanied by appropriate proposals.

If specific actions prove necessary outside the Funds and without prejudice to the measures decided upon within the framework of the other Community policies, such actions may be adopted by the Council acting unanimously on a proposal from the Commission and after consulting the European Parliament, the Economic and Social Committee and the Committee of the Regions.

Article 130c

The European Regional Development Fund is intended to help to redress the main regional imbalances in the Community through participation in the development and structural adjustment of regions whose development is lagging behind and in the conversion of declining industrial regions.

Article 130d

Without prejudice to Article 130e, the Council, acting unanimously on a proposal from the Commission and after obtaining the assent of the European Parliament and consulting the Economic and Social Committee and the Committee of the Regions, shall define the tasks, priority objectives and the organization of the structural Funds, which may involve grouping the Funds. The Council, acting by the same procedure, shall also define the general rules applicable to them and the provisions necessary to ensure their effectiveness and the coordination of the Funds with one another and with the other existing financial instruments.

The Council, acting in accordance with the same procedure, shall before 31 December 1993 set up a Cohesion Fund to provide a financial contribution to projects in the fields of environment and trans-European networks in the area of transport infrastructure.

Article 130e

Implementing decisions relating to the European Regional Development Fund shall be taken by the Council, acting in accordance with the procedure referred to in Article 189c and after consulting the Economic and Social Committee and the Committee of the Regions.

With regard to the European Agricultural Guidance and Guarantee Fund — Guidance Section, and the European Social Fund, Articles 43 and 125 respectively shall continue to apply.

TITLE XV

RESEARCH AND TECHNOLOGICAL DEVELOPMENT

Article 130f

1. The Community shall have the objective of strengthening the scientific and technological bases of Community industry and encouraging it to become more competitive at international level, while promoting all the research activities deemed necessary by virtue of other Chapters of this Treaty.

2. For this purpose the Community shall, throughout the Community, encourage undertakings, including small and medium-sized undertakings, research centres and universities in their research and technological development activities of high quality; it shall support their efforts to cooperate with one another, aiming, notably, at enabling undertakings to exploit the internal market potential to the full, in particular through the opening up of national public contracts, the definition of common standards and the removal of legal and fiscal obstacles to that cooperation.

3. All Community activities under this Treaty in the area of research and technological development, including demonstration projects, shall be decided on and implemented in accordance with the provisions of this Title.

Article 130g

In pursuing these objectives, the Community shall carry out the following activities, complementing the activities carried out in the Member States:

(a) implementation of research, technological development and demonstration programmes, by promoting cooperation with and between undertakings, research centres and universities;

(b) promotion of cooperation in the field of Community research, technological development and demonstration with third countries and international organizations;

(c) dissemination and optimization of the results of activities in Community research, technological development and demonstration;

(d) stimulation of the training and mobility of researchers in the Community.

Article 130h

1. The Community and the Member States shall coordinate their research and technological development activities so as to ensure that national policies and Community policy are mutually consistent.

2. In close cooperation with the Member States, the Commission may take any useful initiative to promote the coordination referred to in paragraph 1.

Article 130i

1. A multiannual framework programme, setting out all the activities of the Community, shall be adopted by the Council, acting in accordance with the procedure referred to in Article 189b after consulting the Economic and Social Committee. The Council shall act unanimously throughout the procedures referred to in Article 189b.

The framework programme shall:

— establish the scientific and technological objectives to be achieved by the activities provided for in Article 130g and fix the relevant priorities;

— indicate the broad lines of such activities;

— fix the maximum overall amount and the detailed rules for Community financial participation in the framework programme and the respective shares in each of the activities provided for.

2. The framework programme shall be adapted or supplemented as the situation changes.

3. The framework programme shall be implemented through specific programmes developed within each activity. Each specific programme shall define the detailed rules for implementing it, fix its duration and provide for the means deemed necessary. The sum of the amounts deemed necessary, fixed in the specific programmes, may not exceed the overall maximum amount fixed for the framework programme and each activity.

4. The Council, acting by a qualified majority on a proposal from the Commission and after consulting the European Parliament and the Economic and Social Committee, shall adopt the specific programmes.

Article 130j

For the implementation of the multiannual framework programme the Council shall:

— *determine the rules for the participation of undertakings, research centres and universities;*

— *lay down the rules governing the dissemination of research results.*

Article 130k

In implementing the multiannual framework programme, supplementary programmes may be decided on involving the participation of certain Member States only, which shall finance them subject to possible Community participation.

The Council shall adopt the rules applicable to supplementary programmes, particularly as regards the dissemination of knowledge and access by other Member States.

Article 130l

In implementing the multiannual framework programme the Community may make provision, in agreement with the Member States concerned, for participation in research and development programmes undertaken by several Member States, including participation in the structures created for the execution of those programmes.

Article 130m

In implementing the multiannual framework programme the Community may make provision for cooperation in Community research, technological development and demonstration with third countries or international organizations.

The detailed arrangements for such cooperation may be the subject of agreements between the Community and the third parties concerned, which shall be negotiated and concluded in accordance with Article 228.

Article 130n

The Community may set up joint undertakings or any other structure necessary for the efficient execution of Community research, technological development and demonstration programmes.

Article 130o

The Council, acting unanimously on a proposal from the Commission and after consulting the European Parliament and the Economic and Social Committee, shall adopt the provisions referred to in Article 130n.

The Council, acting in accordance with the procedure referred to in Article 189c and after consulting the Economic and Social Committee, shall adopt the provisions referred to in Articles 130j to l. Adoption of the supplementary programmes shall require the agreement of the Member States concerned.

Article 130p

At the beginning of each year the Commission shall send a report to the European Parliament and the Council. The report shall include information on research and technological development activities and the dissemination of results during the previous year, and the work programme for the current year.

TITLE XVI

ENVIRONMENT

Article 130r

1. Community policy on the environment shall contribute to pursuit of the following objectives:

— preserving, protecting and improving the quality of the environment;

— protecting human health;

— prudent and rational utilization of natural resources;

— promoting measures at international level to deal with regional or worldwide environmental problems.

2. Community policy on the environment shall aim at a high level of protection taking into account the diversity of situations in the various regions of the Community. It shall be based on the precautionary principle and on the principles that preventive action should be taken, that environmental damage should as a priority be rectified at source and that the polluter should pay. Environmental protection requirements must be integrated into the definition and implementation of other Community policies.

In this context, harmonization measures answering these requirements shall include, where appropriate, a safeguard clause allowing Member States to take provisional measures, for non-economic environmental reasons, subject to a Community inspection procedure.

3. In preparing its policy on the environment, the Community shall take account of:

— *available scientific and technical data;*

— *environmental conditions in the various regions of the Community;*

— *the potential benefits and costs of action or lack of action;*

— *the economic and social development of the Community as a whole and the balanced development of its regions.*

4. Within their respective spheres of competence, the Community and the Member States shall cooperate with third countries and with the competent international organizations. The arrangements for Community cooperation may be the subject of agreements between the Community and the third parties concerned, which shall be negotiated and concluded in accordance with Article 228.

The previous subparagraph shall be without prejudice to Member States' competence to negotiate in international bodies and to conclude international agreements.

Article 130s

1. The Council, acting in accordance with the procedure referred to in Article 189c and after consulting the Economic and Social Committee, shall decide what action is to be taken by the Community in order to achieve the objectives referred to in Article 130r.

2. By way of derogation from the decision-making procedure provided for in paragraph 1 and without prejudice to Article 100a, the Council, acting unanimously on a proposal from the Commission and after consulting the European Parliament and the Economic and Social Committee, shall adopt:

— *provisions primarily of a fiscal nature;*

— *measures concerning town and country planning, land use with the exception of waste management and measures of a general nature, and management of water resources;*

— *measures significantly affecting a Member State's choice between different energy sources and the general structure of its energy supply.*

The Council may, under the conditions laid down in the preceding subparagraph, define those matters referred to in this paragraph on which decisions are to be taken by a qualified majority.

3. In other areas, general action programmes setting out priority objectives to be attained shall be adopted by the Council, acting in accordance with the procedure referred to in Article 189b and after consulting the Economic and Social Committee.

The Council, acting under the terms of paragraph 1 or paragraph 2 according to the case, shall adopt the measures necessary for the implementation of these programmes.

4. Without prejudice to certain measures of a Community nature, the Member States shall finance and implement the environment policy.

5. Without prejudice to the principle that the polluter should pay, if a measure based on the provisions of paragraph 1 involves costs deemed disproportionate for the public authorities of a Member State, the Council shall, in the act adopting that measure, lay down appropriate provisions in the form of:

— temporary derogations, and/or

— financial support from the Cohesion Fund to be set up no later than 31 December 1993 pursuant to Article 130d.

Article 130t

The protective measures adopted pursuant to Article 130s shall not prevent any Member State from maintaining or introducing more stringent protective measures. Such measures must be compatible with this Treaty. They shall be notified to the Commission.

TITLE XVII

DEVELOPMENT COOPERATION

Article 130u

1. Community policy in the sphere of development cooperation, which shall be complementary to the policies pursued by the Member States, shall foster:

— the sustainable economic and social development of the developing countries, and more particularly the most disadvantaged among them;

— the smooth and gradual integration of the developing countries into the world economy;

— the campaign against poverty in the developing countries.

2. Community policy in this area shall contribute to the general objective of developing and consolidating democracy and the rule of law, and to that of respecting human rights and fundamental freedoms.

3. The Community and the Member States shall comply with the commitments and take account of the objectives they have approved in the context of the United Nations and other competent international organizations.

Article 130v

The Community shall take account of the objectives referred to in Article 130u in the policies that it implements which are likely to affect developing countries.

Article 130w

1. Without prejudice to the other provisions of this Treaty the Council, acting in accordance with the procedure referred to in Article 189c, shall adopt the measures necessary to further the objectives referred to in Article 130u. Such measures may take the form of multiannual programmes.

2. The European Investment Bank shall contribute, under the terms laid down in its Statute, to the implementation of the measures referred to in paragraph 1.

3. The provisions of this Article shall not affect cooperation with the African, Caribbean and Pacific countries in the framework of the ACP-EEC Convention.

Article 130x

1. The Community and the Member States shall coordinate their policies on development cooperation and shall consult each other on their aid programmes, including in international organizations and during international conferences. They may undertake joint action. Member States shall contribute if necessary to the implementation of Community aid programmes.

2. The Commission may take any useful initiative to promote the coordination referred to in paragraph 1.

Article 130y

Within their respective spheres of competence, the Community and the Member States shall cooperate with third countries and with the competent international organizations. The arrangements for Community cooperation may be the subject of agreements between the Community and the third parties concerned, which shall be negotiated and concluded in accordance with Article 228.

The previous paragraph shall be without prejudice to Member States' competence to negotiate in international bodies and to conclude international agreements.'

E — In Part Five 'Institutions of the Community'

(39) Article 137 shall be replaced by the following:

'Article 137

The European Parliament, which shall consist of representatives of the peoples of the States brought together in the Community, shall exercise the powers conferred upon it by this Treaty.'

(40) Paragraph 3 of Article 138 shall be replaced by the following:

'3. The European Parliament shall draw up proposals for elections by direct universal suffrage in accordance with a uniform procedure in all Member States.

The Council shall, acting unanimously after obtaining the assent of the European Parliament, which shall act by a majority of its component members, lay down the appropriate provisions, which it shall recommend to Member States for adoption in accordance with their respective constitutional requirements.'

(41) The following Articles shall be inserted:

'Article 138a

Political parties at European level are important as a factor for integration within the Union. They contribute to forming a European awareness and to expressing the political will of the citizens of the Union.

Article 138b

In so far as provided in this Treaty, the European Parliament shall participate in the process leading up to the adoption of Community acts by exercising its powers under the procedures laid down in Articles 189b and 189c and by giving its assent or delivering advisory opinions.

The European Parliament may, acting by a majority of its members, request the Commission to submit any appropriate proposal on matters on which it considers that a Community act is required for the purpose of implementing this Treaty.

Article 138c

In the course of its duties, the European Parliament may, at the request of a quarter of its members, set up a temporary Committee of Inquiry to investigate, without prejudice to the powers conferred by this Treaty on other institutions or bodies, alleged contraventions or maladministration in the implementation of Community law, except where the alleged facts are being examined before a court and while the case is still subject to legal proceedings.

The temporary Committee of Inquiry shall cease to exist on the submission of its report.

The detailed provisions governing the exercise of the right of inquiry shall be determined by common accord of the European Parliament, the Council and the Commission.

Article 138d

Any citizen of the Union, and any natural or legal person residing or having his registered office in a Member State, shall have the right to address, individually or in association with other citizens or persons, a petition to the European Parliament on a matter which comes within the Community's fields of activity and which affects him directly.

Article 138e

1. The European Parliament shall appoint an Ombudsman empowered to receive complaints from any citizen of the Union or any natural or legal person residing or having his registered office in a Member State concerning instances of maladministration in the activities of the Community institutions or bodies, with the exception of the Court of Justice and the Court of First Instance acting in their judicial role.

In accordance with his duties, the Ombudsman shall conduct inquiries for which he finds grounds, either on his own initiative or on the basis of complaints submitted to him direct or through a member of the European Parliament, except where the alleged facts are or have been the subject of legal proceedings. Where the Ombudsman establishes an instance of maladministration, he shall refer the matter to the institution concerned, which shall have a period of three months in which to inform him of its views. The Ombudsman shall then forward a report to the European Parliament and the institution concerned. The person lodging the complaint shall be informed of the outcome of such inquiries.

The Ombudsman shall submit an annual report to the European Parliament on the outcome of his inquiries.

2. The Ombudsman shall be appointed after each election of the European Parliament for the duration of its term of office. The Ombudsman shall be eligible for reappointment.

The Ombudsman may be dismissed by the Court of Justice at the request of the European Parliament if he no longer fulfils the conditions required for the performance of his duties or if he is guilty of serious misconduct.

3. The Ombudsman shall be completely independent in the performance of his duties. In the performance of those duties he shall neither seek nor take instructions from any body. The Ombudsman may not, during his term of office, engage in any other occupation, whether gainful or not.

4. The European Parliament shall, after seeking an opinion from the Commission and with the approval of the Council acting by a qualified majority, lay down the regulations and general conditions governing the performance of the Ombudsman's duties.'

(42) The second subparagraph of Article 144 shall be supplemented by the following sentence:

'In this case, the term of office of the members of the Commission appointed to replace them shall expire on the date on which the term of office of the members of the Commission obliged to resign as a body would have expired.'

(43) The following Article shall be inserted:

'Article 146

The Council shall consist of a representative of each Member State at ministerial level, authorized to commit the government of that Member State.

The office of President shall be held in turn by each Member State in the Council for a term of six months, in the following order of Member States:

— *for a first cycle of six years: Belgium, Denmark, Germany, Greece, Spain, France, Ireland, Italy, Luxembourg, Netherlands, Portugal, United Kingdom;*

— *for the following cycle of six years: Denmark, Belgium, Greece, Germany, France, Spain, Italy, Ireland, Netherlands, Luxembourg, United Kingdom, Portugal.'*

(44) The following Article shall be inserted:

'Article 147

The Council shall meet when convened by its President on his own initiative or at the request of one of its members or of the Commission.'

(45) Article 149 shall be repealed.

(46) The following Article shall be inserted:

'Article 151

1. A committee consisting of the Permanent Representatives of the Member States shall be responsible for preparing the work of the Council and for carrying out the tasks assigned to it by the Council.

2. The Council shall be assisted by a General Secretariat, under the direction of a Secretary-General. The Secretary-General shall be appointed by the Council acting unanimously.

The Council shall decide on the organization of the General Secretariat.

3. The Council shall adopt its rules of procedure.'

(47) The following Article shall be inserted:

'Article 154

The Council shall, acting by a qualified majority, determine the salaries, allowances and pensions of the President and members of the Commission, and of the President, Judges, Advocates-General and Registrar of the Court of Justice. It shall also, again by a qualified majority, determine any payment to be made instead of remuneration.'

(48) The following Articles shall be inserted:

'Article 156

The Commission shall publish annually, not later than one month before the opening of the session of the European Parliament, a general report on the activities of the Community.

Article 157

1. The Commission shall consist of 17 members, who shall be chosen on the grounds of their general competence and whose independence is beyond doubt.

The number of members of the Commission may be altered by the Council, acting unanimously.

Only nationals of Member States may be members of the Commission.

The Commission must include at least one national of each of the Member States, but may not include more than two members having the nationality of the same State.

2. The members of the Commission shall, in the general interest of the Community, be completely independent in the performance of their duties.

In the performance of these duties, they shall neither seek nor take instructions from any government or from any other body. They shall refrain from any action incompatible with their duties. Each Member State undertakes to respect this principle and not to seek to influence the members of the Commission in the performance of their tasks.

The members of the Commission may not, during their term of office, engage in any other occupation, whether gainful or not. When entering upon their duties they shall give a solemn undertaking that, both during and after their term of office, they will respect the obligations arising therefrom and in particular their duty to behave with integrity and discretion as regards the acceptance, after they have ceased to hold office, of certain appointments or benefits. In the event of any breach of these obligations, the Court of Justice may, on application by the Council or the Commission, rule that the member concerned be, according to the circumstances, either compulsorily retired in accordance with Article 160 or deprived of his right to a pension or other benefits in its stead.

Article 158

1. The members of the Commission shall be appointed, in accordance with the procedure referred to in paragraph 2, for a period of five years, subject, if need be, to Article 144.

Their term of office shall be renewable.

2. The governments of the Member States shall nominate by common accord, after consulting the European Parliament, the person they intend to appoint as President of the Commission.

The governments of the Member States shall, in consultation with the nominee for President, nominate the other persons whom they intend to appoint as members of the Commission.

The President and the other members of the Commission thus nominated shall be subject as a body to a vote of approval by the European Parliament. After approval by the European Parliament, the President and the other members of the Commission shall be appointed by common accord of the governments of the Member States.

3. Paragraphs 1 and 2 shall be applied for the first time to the President and the other members of the Commission whose term of office begins on 7 January 1995.

The President and the other members of the Commission whose term of office begins on 7 January 1993 shall be appointed by common accord of the governments of the Member States. Their term of office shall expire on 6 January 1995.

Article 159

Apart from normal replacement, or death, the duties of a member of the Commission shall end when he resigns or is compulsorily retired.

The vacancy thus caused shall be filled for the remainder of the member's term of office by a new member appointed by common accord of the governments of the Member States. The Council may, acting unanimously, decide that such a vacancy need not be filled.

In the event of resignation, compulsory retirement or death, the President shall be replaced for the remainder of his term of office. The procedure laid down in Article 158(2) shall be applicable for the replacement of the President.

Save in the case of compulsory retirement under Article 160, members of the Commission shall remain in office until they have been replaced.

Article 160

If any member of the Commission no longer fulfils the conditions required for the performance of his duties or if he has been guilty of serious misconduct, the Court of Justice may, on application by the Council or the Commission, compulsorily retire him.

Article 161

The Commission may appoint a Vice-President or two Vice-Presidents from among its members.

Article 162

1. The Council and the Commission shall consult each other and shall settle by common accord their methods of cooperation.

2. The Commission shall adopt its rules of procedure so as to ensure that both it and its departments operate in accordance with the provisions of this Treaty. It shall ensure that these rules are published.

Article 163

The Commission shall act by a majority of the number of members provided for in Article 157.

A meeting of the Commission shall be valid only if the number of members laid down in its rules of procedure is present.'

(49) Article 165 shall be replaced by the following:

'Article 165

The Court of Justice shall consist of 13 Judges.

The Court of Justice shall sit in plenary session. It may, however, form chambers, each consisting of three or five Judges, either to undertake certain preparatory inquiries or to adjudicate on particular categories of cases in accordance with rules laid down for these purposes.

The Court of Justice shall sit in plenary session when a Member State or a Community institution that is a party to the proceedings so requests.

Should the Court of Justice so request, the Council may, acting unanimously, increase the number of Judges and make the necessary adjustments to the second and third paragraphs of this Article and to the second paragraph of Article 167.'

(50) Article 168a shall be replaced by the following:

'Article 168a

1. A Court of First Instance shall be attached to the Court of Justice with jurisdiction to hear and determine at first instance, subject to a right of appeal to the Court of Justice on points of law only and in accordance with the conditions laid down by the Statute, certain classes of action or proceeding defined in accordance with the conditions laid down in paragraph 2. The Court of First Instance shall not be competent to hear and determine questions referred for a preliminary ruling under Article 177.

2. At the request of the Court of Justice and after consulting the European Parliament and the Commission, the Council, acting unanimously, shall determine the classes of action or proceeding referred to in paragraph 1 and the composition of the Court of First Instance and shall adopt the necessary adjustments and additional provisions to the Statute of the Court of Justice. Unless the Council decides otherwise, the provisions of this Treaty relating to the Court of Justice, in particular the provisions of the Protocol on the Statute of the Court of Justice, shall apply to the Court of First Instance.

3. The members of the Court of First Instance shall be chosen from persons whose independence is beyond doubt and who possess the ability required for appointment to judicial office; they shall be appointed by common accord of the governments of the Member States for a term of six years. The membership shall be partially renewed every three years. Retiring members shall be eligible for reappointment.

4. The Court of First Instance shall establish its rules of procedure in agreement with the Court of Justice. Those rules shall require the unanimous approval of the Council.'

(51) Article 171 shall be replaced by the following:

'Article 171

1. If the Court of Justice finds that a Member State has failed to fulfil an obligation under this Treaty, the State shall be required to take the necessary measures to comply with the judgment of the Court of Justice.

2. If the Commission considers that the Member State concerned has not taken such measures it shall, after giving that State the opportunity to submit its observations, issue a reasoned opinion specifying the points on which the Member State concerned has not complied with the judgment of the Court of Justice.

If the Member State concerned fails to take the necessary measures to comply with the Court's judgment within the time-limit laid down by the Commission, the latter may bring the case before the Court of Justice. In so doing it shall specify the amount of the lump sum or penalty payment to be paid by the Member State concerned which it considers appropriate in the circumstances.

If the Court of Justice finds that the Member State concerned has not complied with its judgment it may impose a lump sum or penalty payment on it.

This procedure shall be without prejudice to Article 170.'

(52) Article 172 shall be replaced by the following:

'*Article 172*

Regulations adopted jointly by the European Parliament and the Council, and by the Council, pursuant to the provisions of this Treaty, may give the Court of Justice unlimited jurisdiction with regard to the penalties provided for in such regulations.'

(53) Article 173 shall be replaced by the following:

'*Article 173*

The Court of Justice shall review the legality of acts adopted jointly by the European Parliament and the Council, of acts of the Council, of the Commission and of the ECB, other than recommendations and opinions, and of acts of the European Parliament intended to produce legal effects vis-à-vis *third parties.*

It shall for this purpose have jurisdiction in actions brought by a Member State, the Council or the Commission on grounds of lack of competence, infringement of an essential procedural requirement, infringement of this Treaty or of any rule of law relating to its application, or misuse of powers.

The Court shall have jurisdiction under the same conditions in actions brought by the European Parliament and by the ECB for the purpose of protecting their prerogatives.

Any natural or legal person may, under the same conditions, institute proceedings against a decision addressed to that person or against a decision which, although in the form of a regulation or a decision addressed to another person, is of direct and individual concern to the former.

The proceedings provided for in this Article shall be instituted within two months of the publication of the measure, or of its notification to the plaintiff, or, in the absence thereof, of the day on which it came to the knowledge of the latter, as the case may be.'

(54) Article 175 shall be replaced by the following:

'Article 175

Should the European Parliament, the Council or the Commission, in infringement of this Treaty, fail to act, the Member States and the other institutions of the Community may bring an action before the Court of Justice to have the infringement established.

The action shall be admissible only if the institution concerned has first been called upon to act. If, within two months of being so called upon, the institution concerned has not defined its position, the action may be brought within a further period of two months.

Any natural or legal person may, under the conditions laid down in the preceding paragraphs, complain to the Court of Justice that an institution of the Community has failed to address to that person any act other than a recommendation or an opinion.

The Court of Justice shall have jurisdiction, under the same conditions, in actions or proceedings brought by the ECB in the areas falling within the latter's field of competence and in actions or proceedings brought against the latter.'

(55) Article 176 shall be replaced by the following:

'Article 176

The institution or institutions whose act has been declared void or whose failure to act has been declared contrary to this Treaty shall be required to take the necessary measures to comply with the judgment of the Court of Justice.

This obligation shall not affect any obligation which may result from the application of the second paragraph of Article 215.

This Article shall also apply to the ECB.'

(56) Article 177 shall be replaced by the following:

'Article 177

The Court of Justice shall have jurisdiction to give preliminary rulings concerning:

(a) the interpretation of this Treaty;

(b) the validity and interpretation of acts of the institutions of the Community and of the ECB;

(c) the interpretation of the statutes of bodies established by an act of the Council, where those statutes so provide.

Where such a question is raised before any court or tribunal of a Member State, that court or tribunal may, if it considers that a decision on the question is necessary to enable it to give judgment, request the Court of Justice to give a ruling thereon.

Where any such question is raised in a case pending before a court or tribunal of a Member State against whose decisions there is no judicial remedy under national law, that court or tribunal shall bring the matter before the Court of Justice.'

(57) Article 180 shall be replaced by the following:

'Article 180

The Court of Justice shall, within the limits hereinafter laid down, have jurisdiction in disputes concerning:

(a) the fulfilment by Member States of obligations under the Statute of the European Investment Bank. In this connection, the Board of Directors of the Bank shall enjoy the powers conferred upon the Commission by Article 169;

(b) measures adopted by the Board of Governors of the European Investment Bank. In this connection, any Member State, the Commission or the Board of Directors of the Bank may institute proceedings under the conditions laid down in Article 173;

(c) measures adopted by the Board of Directors of the European Investment Bank. Proceedings against such measures may be instituted only by Member States or by the Commission, under the conditions laid down in Article 173, and solely on the grounds of non-compliance with the procedure provided for in Article 21(2), (5), (6) and (7) of the Statute of the Bank;

(d) the fulfilment by national central banks of obligations under this Treaty and the Statute of the ESCB. In this connection the powers of the Council of the ECB in respect of national central banks shall be the same as those conferred upon the Commission in respect of Member States by Article 169. If the Court of Justice finds that a national central bank has failed to fulfil an obligation under this Treaty, that bank shall be required to take the necessary measures to comply with the judgment of the Court of Justice.'

(58) Article 184 shall be replaced by the following:

'Article 184

Notwithstanding the expiry of the period laid down in the fifth paragraph of Article 173, any party may, in proceedings in which a regulation adopted jointly by the European Parliament and the Council, or a regulation of the Council, of the Commission, or of the ECB is at issue, plead the grounds specified in the second paragraph of Article 173 in order to invoke before the Court of Justice the inapplicability of that regulation.'

(59) The following section shall be inserted:

'SECTION 5

The Court of Auditors

Article 188a

The Court of Auditors shall carry out the audit.

Article 188b

1. The Court of Auditors shall consist of 12 members.

2. The members of the Court of Auditors shall be chosen from among persons who belong or have belonged in their respective countries to external audit bodies or who are especially qualified for this office. Their independence must be beyond doubt.

3. The members of the Court of Auditors shall be appointed for a term of six years by the Council, acting unanimously after consulting the European Parliament.

However, when the first appointments are made, four members of the Court of Auditors, chosen by lot, shall be appointed for a term of office of four years only.

The members of the Court of Auditors shall be eligible for reappointment.

They shall elect the President of the Court of Auditors from among their number for a term of three years. The President may be re-elected.

4. The members of the Court of Auditors shall, in the general interest of the Community, be completely independent in the performance of their duties.

In the performance of these duties, they shall neither seek nor take instructions from any government or from any other body. They shall refrain from any action incompatible with their duties.

5. The members of the Court of Auditors may not, during their term of office, engage in any other occupation, whether gainful or not. When entering upon their duties they shall give a solemn undertaking that, both during and after their term of office, they will respect the obligations arising therefrom and in particular their duty to behave with integrity and discretion as regards the acceptance, after they have ceased to hold office, of certain appointments or benefits.

6. Apart from normal replacement, or death, the duties of a member of the Court of Auditors shall end when he resigns, or is compulsorily retired by a ruling of the Court of Justice pursuant to paragraph 7.

The vacancy thus caused shall be filled for the remainder of the member's term of office.

Save in the case of compulsory retirement, members of the Court of Auditors shall remain in office until they have been replaced.

7. A member of the Court of Auditors may be deprived of his office or of his right to a pension or other benefits in its stead only if the Court of Justice, at the request of the Court of Auditors, finds that he no longer fulfils the requisite conditions or meets the obligations arising from his office.

8. The Council, acting by a qualified majority, shall determine the conditions of employment of the President and the members of the Court of Auditors and in particular their salaries, allowances and pensions. It shall also, by the same majority, determine any payment to be made instead of remuneration.

9. The provisions of the Protocol on the Privileges and Immunities of the European Communities applicable to the Judges of the Court of Justice shall also apply to the members of the Court of Auditors.

Article 188c

1. The Court of Auditors shall examine the accounts of all revenue and expenditure of the Community. It shall also examine the accounts of all revenue and expenditure of all bodies set up by the Community in so far as the relevant constituent instrument does not preclude such examination.

The Court of Auditors shall provide the European Parliament and the Council with a statement of assurance as to the reliability of the accounts and the legality and regularity of the underlying transactions.

2. *The Court of Auditors shall examine whether all revenue has been received and all expenditure incurred in a lawful and regular manner and whether the financial management has been sound.*

The audit of revenue shall be carried out on the basis both of the amounts established as due and the amounts actually paid to the Community.

The audit of expenditure shall be carried out on the basis both of commitments undertaken and payments made.

These audits may be carried out before the closure of accounts for the financial year in question.

3. *The audit shall be based on records and, if necessary, performed on the spot in the other institutions of the Community and in the Member States. In the Member States the audit shall be carried out in liaison with the national audit bodies or, if these do not have the necessary powers, with the competent national departments. These bodies or departments shall inform the Court of Auditors whether they intend to take part in the audit.*

The other institutions of the Community and the national audit bodies or, if these do not have the necessary powers, the competent national departments, shall forward to the Court of Auditors, at its request, any document or information necessary to carry out its task.

4. *The Court of Auditors shall draw up an annual report after the close of each financial year. It shall be forwarded to the other institutions of the Community and shall be published, together with the replies of these institutions to the observations of the Court of Auditors, in the* Official Journal of the European Communities.

The Court of Auditors may also, at any time, submit observations, particularly in the form of special reports, on specific questions and deliver opinions at the request of one of the other institutions of the Community.

It shall adopt its annual reports, special reports or opinions by a majority of its members.

It shall assist the European Parliament and the Council in exercising their powers of control over the implementation of the budget.'

(60) Article 189 shall be replaced by the following:

'Article 189

In order to carry out their task and in accordance with the provisions of this Treaty, the European Parliament acting jointly with the Council, the Council and the Commission shall make regulations and issue directives, take decisions, make recommendations or deliver opinions.

A regulation shall have general application. It shall be binding in its entirety and directly applicable in all Member States.

A directive shall be binding, as to the result to be achieved, upon each Member State to which it is addressed, but shall leave to the national authorities the choice of form and methods.

A decision shall be binding in its entirety upon those to whom it is addressed.

Recommendations and opinions shall have no binding force.'

(61) The following Articles shall be inserted:

'Article 189a

1. Where, in pursuance of this Treaty, the Council acts on a proposal from the Commission, unanimity shall be required for an act constituting an amendment to that proposal, subject to Article 189b(4) and (5).

2. As long as the Council has not acted, the Commission may alter its proposal at any time during the procedures leading to the adoption of a Community act.

Article 189b

1. Where reference is made in this Treaty to this Article for the adoption of an act, the following procedure shall apply.

2. The Commission shall submit a proposal to the European Parliament and the Council.

The Council, acting by a qualified majority after obtaining the opinion of the European Parliament, shall adopt a common position. The common position shall be communicated to the European Parliament. The Council shall inform the European Parliament fully of the reasons which led it to adopt its common position. The Commission shall inform the European Parliament fully of its position.

If, within three months of such communication, the European Parliament:

(a) approves the common position, the Council shall definitively adopt the act in question in accordance with that common position;

(b) has not taken a decision, the Council shall adopt the act in question in accordance with its common position;

(c) indicates, by an absolute majority of its component members, that it intends to reject the common position, it shall immediately inform the Council. The Council may convene a meeting of the Conciliation Committee referred to in paragraph 4 to explain further its position. The European Parliament shall thereafter either confirm, by an absolute majority of its component members, its rejection of the common position, in which event the proposed act shall be deemed not to have been adopted, or propose amendments in accordance with subparagraph (d) of this paragraph;

(d) proposes amendments to the common position by an absolute majority of its component members, the amended text shall be forwarded to the Council and to the Commission, which shall deliver an opinion on those amendments.

3. If, within three months of the matter being referred to it, the Council, acting by a qualified majority, approves all the amendments of the European Parliament, it shall amend its common position accordingly and adopt the act in question; however, the Council shall act unanimously on the amendments on which the Commission has delivered a negative opinion. If the Council does not approve the act in question, the President of the Council, in agreement with the President of the European Parliament, shall forthwith convene a meeting of the Conciliation Committee.

4. The Conciliation Committee, which shall be composed of the members of the Council or their representatives and an equal number of representatives of the European Parliament, shall have the task of reaching agreement on a joint text, by a qualified majority of the members of the Council or their representatives and by a majority of the representatives of the European Parliament. The Commission shall take part in the Conciliation Committee's proceedings and shall take all the necessary initiatives with a view to reconciling the positions of the European Parliament and the Council.

5. If, within six weeks of its being convened, the Conciliation Committee approves a joint text, the European Parliament, acting by an absolute majority of the votes cast, and the Council, acting by a qualified majority, shall have a period of six weeks from that approval in which to adopt the act in question in accordance with the joint text. If one of the two institutions fails to approve the proposed act, it shall be deemed not to have been adopted.

6. Where the Conciliation Committee does not approve a joint text, the proposed act shall be deemed not to have been adopted unless the Council, acting by a qualified majority within six weeks of expiry of the period granted to the Conciliation Committee, confirms the common position to which it agreed before the conciliation procedure was initiated, possibly with amendments proposed by the

European Parliament. In this case, the act in question shall be finally adopted unless the European Parliament, within six weeks of the date of confirmation by the Council, rejects the text by an absolute majority of its component members, in which case the proposed act shall be deemed not to have been adopted.

7. The periods of three months and six weeks referred to in this Article may be extended by a maximum of one month and two weeks respectively by common accord of the European Parliament and the Council. The period of three months referred to in paragraph 2 shall be automatically extended by two months where paragraph 2(c) applies.

8. The scope of the procedure under this Article may be widened, in accordance with the procedure provided for in Article N (2) of the Treaty on European Union, on the basis of a report to be submitted to the Council by the Commission by 1996 at the latest.

Article 189c

Where reference is made in this Treaty to this Article for the adoption of an act, the following procedure shall apply:

(a) The Council, acting by a qualified majority on a proposal from the Commission and after obtaining the opinion of the European Parliament, shall adopt a common position.

(b) The Council's common position shall be communicated to the European Parliament. The Council and the Commission shall inform the European Parliament fully of the reasons which led the Council to adopt its common position and also of the Commission's position.

If, within three months of such communication, the European Parliament approves this common position or has not taken a decision within that period, the Council shall definitively adopt the act in question in accordance with the common position.

(c) The European Parliament may, within the period of three months referred to in subparagraph (b), by an absolute majority of its component members, propose amendments to the Council's common position. The European Parliament may also, by the same majority, reject the Council's common position. The result of the proceedings shall be transmitted to the Council and the Commission.

If the European Parliament has rejected the Council's common position, unanimity shall be required for the Council to act on a second reading.

(d) The Commission shall, within a period of one month, re-examine the proposal on the basis of which the Council adopted its common position, by taking into account the amendments proposed by the European Parliament.

The Commission shall forward to the Council, at the same time as its re-examined proposal, the amendments of the European Parliament which it has not accepted, and shall express its opinion on them. The Council may adopt these amendments unanimously.

(e) *The Council, acting by a qualified majority, shall adopt the proposal as re-examined by the Commission.*

Unanimity shall be required for the Council to amend the proposal as re-examined by the Commission.

(f) *In the cases referred to in subparagraphs (c), (d) and (e), the Council shall be required to act within a period of three months. If no decision is taken within this period, the Commission proposal shall be deemed not to have been adopted.*

(g) *The periods referred to in subparagraphs (b) and (f) may be extended by a maximum of one month by common accord between the Council and the European Parliament.'*

(62) Article 190 shall be replaced by the following:

'Article 190

Regulations, directives and decisions adopted jointly by the European Parliament and the Council, and such acts adopted by the Council or the Commission, shall state the reasons on which they are based and shall refer to any proposals or opinions which were required to be obtained pursuant to this Treaty.'

(63) Article 191 shall be replaced by the following:

'Article 191

1. Regulations, directives and decisions adopted in accordance with the procedure referred to in Article 189b shall be signed by the President of the European Parliament and by the President of the Council and published in the Official Journal of the European Communities. *They shall enter into force on the date specified in them or, in the absence thereof, on the 20th day following that of their publication.*

2. Regulations of the Council and of the Commission, as well as directives of those institutions which are addressed to all Member States, shall be published in the Official Journal of the European Communities. *They shall enter into force on the date specified in them or, in the absence thereof, on the 20th day following that of their publication.*

3. Other directives, and decisions, shall be notified to those to whom they are addressed and shall take effect upon such notification.'

(64) Article 194 shall be replaced by the following:

'*Article 194*

The number of members of the Economic and Social Committee shall be as follows:

Belgium	*12*
Denmark	*9*
Germany	*24*
Greece	*12*
Spain	*21*
France	*24*
Ireland	*9*
Italy	*24*
Luxembourg	*6*
Netherlands	*12*
Portugal	*12*
United Kingdom	*24*

The members of the Committee shall be appointed by the Council, acting unanimously, for four years. Their appointments shall be renewable.

The members of the Committee may not be bound by any mandatory instructions. They shall be completely independent in the performance of their duties, in the general interest of the Community.

The Council, acting by a qualified majority, shall determine the allowances of members of the Committee.'

(65) Article 196 shall be replaced by the following:

'*Article 196*

The Committee shall elect its chairman and officers from among its members for a term of two years.

It shall adopt its rules of procedure.

The Committee shall be convened by its chairman at the request of the Council or of the Commission. It may also meet on its own initiative.'

(66) Article 198 shall be replaced by the following:

'Article 198

The Committee must be consulted by the Council or by the Commission where this Treaty so provides. The Committee may be consulted by these institutions in all cases in which they consider it appropriate. It may issue an opinion on its own initiative in cases in which it considers such action appropriate.

The Council or the Commission shall, if it considers it necessary, set the Committee, for the submission of its opinion, a time-limit which may not be less than one month from the date on which the chairman receives notification to this effect. Upon expiry of the time-limit, the absence of an opinion shall not prevent further action.

The opinion of the Committee and that of the specialized section, together with a record of the proceedings, shall be forwarded to the Council and to the Commission.'

(67) The following Chapter shall be inserted:

'CHAPTER 4

The Committee of the Regions

Article 198a

A Committee consisting of representatives of regional and local bodies, here-inafter referred to as "the Committee of the Regions", is hereby established with advisory status.

The number of members of the Committee of the Regions shall be as follows:

Belgium	*12*
Denmark	*9*
Germany	*24*
Greece	*12*
Spain	*21*
France	*24*
Ireland	*9*
Italy	*24*
Luxembourg	*6*
Netherlands	*12*
Portugal	*12*
United Kingdom	*24*

The members of the Committee and an equal number of alternate members shall be appointed for four years by the Council acting unanimously on proposals from the respective Member States. Their term of office shall be renewable.

The members of the Committee may not be bound by any mandatory instructions. They shall be completely independent in the performance of their duties, in the general interest of the Community.

Article 198b

The Committee of the Regions shall elect its chairman and officers from among its members for a term of two years.

It shall adopt its rules of procedure and shall submit them for approval to the Council, acting unanimously.

The Committee shall be convened by its chairman at the request of the Council or of the Commission. It may also meet on its own initiative.

Article 198c

The Committee of the Regions shall be consulted by the Council or by the Commission where this Treaty so provides and in all other cases in which one of these two institutions considers it appropriate.

The Council or the Commission shall, if it considers it necessary, set the Committee, for the submission of its opinion, a time-limit which may not be less than one month from the date on which the chairman receives notification to this effect. Upon expiry of the time-limit, the absence of an opinion shall not prevent further action.

Where the Economic and Social Committee is consulted pursuant to Article 198, the Committee of the Regions shall be informed by the Council or the Commission of the request for an opinion. Where it considers that specific regional interests are involved, the Committee of the Regions may issue an opinion on the matter.

It may issue an opinion on its own initiative in cases in which it considers such action appropriate.

The opinion of the Committee, together with a record of the proceedings, shall be forwarded to the Council and to the Commission.'

(68) The following chapter shall be inserted:

'CHAPTER 5

European Investment Bank

Article 198d

The European Investment Bank shall have legal personality.

The members of the European Investment Bank shall be the Member States.

The Statute of the European Investment Bank is laid down in a Protocol annexed to this Treaty.

Article 198e

The task of the European Investment Bank shall be to contribute, by having recourse to the capital market and utilizing its own resources, to the balanced and steady development of the common market in the interest of the Community. For this purpose the Bank shall, operating on a non-profit-making basis, grant loans and give guarantees which facilitate the financing of the following projects in all sectors of the economy:

(a) projects for developing less-developed regions;

(b) projects for modernizing or converting undertakings or for developing fresh activities called for by the progressive establishment of the common market, where these projects are of such a size or nature that they cannot be entirely financed by the various means available in the individual Member States;

(c) projects of common interest to several Member States which are of such a size or nature that they cannot be entirely financed by the various means available in the individual Member States.

In carrying out its task, the Bank shall facilitate the financing of investment programmes in conjunction with assistance from the structural Funds and other Community financial instruments.'

(69) Article 199 shall be replaced by the following:

'Article 199

All items of revenue and expenditure of the Community, including those relating to the European Social Fund, shall be included in estimates to be drawn up for each financial year and shall be shown in the budget.

Administrative expenditure occasioned for the institutions by the provisions of the Treaty on European Union relating to common foreign and security policy and to cooperation in the fields of justice and home affairs shall be charged to the budget. The operational expenditure occasioned by the implementation of the said provisions may, under the conditions referred to therein, be charged to the budget.

The revenue and expenditure shown in the budget shall be in balance.'

(70) Article 200 shall be repealed.

(71) Article 201 shall be replaced by the following:

'Article 201

Without prejudice to other revenue, the budget shall be financed wholly from own resources.

The Council, acting unanimously on a proposal from the Commission and after consulting the European Parliament, shall lay down provisions relating to the system of own resources of the Community, which it shall recommend to the Member States for adoption in accordance with their respective constitutional requirements.'

(72) The following Article shall be inserted:

'Article 201a

With a view to maintaining budgetary discipline, the Commission shall not make any proposal for a Community act, or alter its proposals, or adopt any implementing measure which is likely to have appreciable implications for the budget without providing the assurance that that proposal or that measure is capable of being financed within the limit of the Community's own resources arising under provisions laid down by the Council pursuant to Article 201.'

(73) Article 205 shall be replaced by the following:

'Article 205

The Commission shall implement the budget, in accordance with the provisions of the regulations made pursuant to Article 209, on its own responsibility and within the limits of the appropriations, having regard to the principles of sound financial management.

The regulations shall lay down detailed rules for each institution concerning its part in effecting its own expenditure.

Within the budget, the Commission may, subject to the limits and conditions laid down in the regulations made pursuant to Article 209, transfer appropriations from one chapter to another or from one subdivision to another.'

(74) Article 206 shall be replaced by the following:

'Article 206

1. The European Parliament, acting on a recommendation from the Council which shall act by a qualified majority, shall give a discharge to the Commission in respect of the implementation of the budget. To this end, the Council and the European Parliament in turn shall examine the accounts and the financial statement referred to in Article 205a, the annual report by the Court of Auditors together with the replies of the institutions under audit to the observations of the Court of Auditors and any relevant special reports by the Court of Auditors.

2. Before giving a discharge to the Commission, or for any other purpose in connection with the exercise of its powers over the implementation of the budget, the European Parliament may ask to hear the Commission give evidence with regard to the execution of expenditure or the operation of financial control systems. The Commission shall submit any necessary information to the European Parliament at the latter's request.

3. The Commission shall take all appropriate steps to act on the observations in the decisions giving discharge and on other observations by the European Parliament relating to the execution of expenditure, as well as on comments accompanying the recommendations on discharge adopted by the Council.

At the request of the European Parliament or the Council, the Commission shall report on the measures taken in the light of these observations and comments and in particular on the instructions given to the departments which are responsible for the implementation of the budget. These reports shall also be forwarded to the Court of Auditors.'

(75) Articles 206a and 206b shall be repealed.

(76) Article 209 shall be replaced by the following:

'Article 209

The Council, acting unanimously on a proposal from the Commission and after consulting the European Parliament and obtaining the opinion of the Court of Auditors, shall:

(a) make Financial Regulations specifying in particular the procedure to be adopted for establishing and implementing the budget and for presenting and auditing accounts;

(b) determine the methods and procedure whereby the budget revenue provided under the arrangements relating to the Community's own resources shall be made available to the Commission, and determine the measures to be applied, if need be, to meet cash requirements;

(c) lay down rules concerning the responsibility of financial controllers, authorizing officers and accounting officers, and concerning appropriate arrangements for inspection.'

(77) The following Article shall be inserted:

'Article 209a

Member States shall take the same measures to counter fraud affecting the financial interests of the Community as they take to counter fraud affecting their own financial interests.

Without prejudice to other provisions of this Treaty, Member States shall coordinate their action aimed at protecting the financial interests of the Community against fraud. To this end they shall organize, with the help of the Commission, close and regular cooperation between the competent departments of their administrations.'

(78) Article 215 shall be replaced by the following:

'Article 215

The contractual liability of the Community shall be governed by the law applicable to the contract in question.

In the case of non-contractual liability, the Community shall, in accordance with the general principles common to the laws of the Member States, make good any damage caused by its institutions or by its servants in the performance of their duties.

The preceding paragraph shall apply under the same conditions to damage caused by the ECB or by its servants in the performance of their duties.

The personal liability of its servants towards the Community shall be governed by the provisions laid down in their Staff Regulations or in the Conditions of Employment applicable to them.'

(79) Article 227 shall be amended as follows:

(a) paragraph 2 shall be replaced by the following:

'2. With regard to the French overseas departments, the general and particular provisions of this Treaty relating to:

— the free movement of goods;

— agriculture, save for Article 40(4);

— the liberalization of services;

— the rules on competition;

— the protective measures provided for in Articles 109h, 109i and 226;

— the institutions,

shall apply as soon as this Treaty enters into force.

The conditions under which the other provisions of this Treaty are to apply shall be determined, within two years of the entry into force of this Treaty, by decisions of the Council, acting unanimously on a proposal from the Commission.

The institutions of the Community will, within the framework of the procedures provided for in this Treaty, in particular Article 226, take care that the economic and social development of these areas is made possible.';

(b) in paragraph 5, subparagraph (a) shall be replaced by the following:

'(a) this Treaty shall not apply to the Faeroe Islands.'

(80) Article 228 shall be replaced by the following:

'Article 228

1. Where this Treaty provides for the conclusion of agreements between the Community and one or more States or international organizations, the Commission shall make recommendations to the Council, which shall authorize the Commission to open the necessary negotiations. The Commission shall conduct these negotiations in consultation with special committees appointed by the Council to assist it in this task and within the framework of such directives as the Council may issue to it.

In exercising the powers conferred upon it by this paragraph, the Council shall act by a qualified majority, except in the cases provided for in the second sentence of paragraph 2, for which it shall act unanimously.

2. Subject to the powers vested in the Commission in this field, the agreements shall be concluded by the Council, acting by a qualified majority on a proposal from the Commission. The Council shall act unanimously when the agreement covers a field for which unanimity is required for the adoption of internal rules, and for the agreements referred to in Article 238.

3. The Council shall conclude agreements after consulting the European Parliament, except for the agreements referred to in Article 113(3), including cases where the agreement covers a field for which the procedure referred to in Article 189b or that referred to in Article 189c is required for the adoption of internal rules. The European Parliament shall deliver its opinion within a time-limit which the Council may lay down according to the urgency of the matter. In the absence of an opinion within that time-limit, the Council may act.

By way of derogation from the previous subparagraph, agreements referred to in Article 238, other agreements establishing a specific institutional framework by organizing cooperation procedures, agreements having important budgetary implications for the Community and agreements entailing amendment of an act adopted under the procedure referred to in Article 189b shall be concluded after the assent of the European Parliament has been obtained.

The Council and the European Parliament may, in an urgent situation, agree upon a time-limit for the assent.

4. When concluding an agreement, the Council may, by way of derogation from paragraph 2, authorize the Commission to approve modifications on behalf of the Community where the agreement provides for them to be adopted by a simplified procedure or by a body set up by the agreement; it may attach specific conditions to such authorization.

5. When the Council envisages concluding an agreement which calls for amendments to this Treaty, the amendments must first be adopted in accordance with the procedure laid down in Article N of the Treaty on European Union.

6. The Council, the Commission or a Member State may obtain the opinion of the Court of Justice as to whether an agreement envisaged is compatible with the provisions of this Treaty. Where the opinion of the Court of Justice is adverse, the agreement may enter into force only in accordance with Article N of the Treaty on European Union.

7. Agreements concluded under the conditions set out in this Article shall be binding on the institutions of the Community and on Member States.'

(81) The following Article shall be inserted:

'Article 228a

Where it is provided, in a common position or in a joint action adopted according to the provisions of the Treaty on European Union relating to the common foreign and security policy, for an action by the Community to interrupt or to reduce, in part or completely, economic relations with one or more third countries, the Council shall take the necessary urgent measures. The Council shall act by a qualified majority on a proposal from the Commission.'

(82) Article 231 shall be replaced by the following:

'Article 231

The Community shall establish close cooperation with the Organization for Economic Cooperation and Development, the details of which shall be determined by common accord.'

(83) Articles 236 and 237 shall be repealed.

(84) Article 238 shall be replaced by the following:

'Article 238

The Community may conclude with one or more States or international organizations agreements establishing an association involving reciprocal rights and obligations, common action and special procedures.'

F — In Annex III:

(85) The title shall be replaced by the following:

'List of invisible transactions referred to in Article 73h of this Treaty'.

G — In the Protocol on the Statute of the European Investment Bank:

(86) The reference to Articles 129 and 130 shall be replaced by a reference to Articles 198d and 198e.

TITLE III

PROVISIONS AMENDING THE TREATY ESTABLISHING THE EUROPEAN COAL AND STEEL COMMUNITY

Article H

The Treaty establishing the European Coal and Steel Community shall be amended in accordance with the provisions of this Article.

(1) Article 7 shall be replaced by the following:

'Article 7

The institutions of the Community shall be:

— *a HIGH AUTHORITY (hereinafter referred to as "the Commission");*

— *a COMMON ASSEMBLY (hereinafter referred to as "the European Parliament");*

— *a SPECIAL COUNCIL OF MINISTERS (hereinafter referred to as "the Council");*

— *a COURT OF JUSTICE;*

— *a COURT OF AUDITORS.*

The Commission shall be assisted by a Consultative Committee.'

(2) The following Articles shall be inserted:

'Article 9

1. The Commission shall consist of 17 members, who shall be chosen on the grounds of their general competence and whose independence is beyond doubt.

The number of members of the Commission may be altered by the Council, acting unanimously.

Only nationals of the Member States may be members of the Commission.

The Commission must include at least one national of each of the Member States, but may not include more than two members having the nationality of the same State.

2. The members of the Commission shall, in the general interest of the Community, be completely independent in the performance of their duties.

In the performance of these duties, they shall neither seek nor take instructions from any government or from any other body. They shall refrain from any action incompatible with their duties. Each Member State undertakes to respect this principle and not to seek to influence the members of the Commission in the performance of their tasks.

The members of the Commission may not, during their term of office, engage in any other occupation, whether gainful or not. When entering upon their duties they shall give a solemn undertaking that, both during and after their term of office, they will respect the obligations arising therefrom and in particular their duty to behave with integrity and discretion as regards the acceptance, after they have ceased to hold office, of certain appointments or benefits. In the event of any breach of these obligations, the Court of Justice may, on application by the Council or the Commission, rule that the member concerned be, according to the circumstances, either compulsorily retired in accordance with Article 12a or deprived of his right to a pension or other benefits in its stead.

Article 10

1. The members of the Commission shall be appointed, in accordance with the procedure referred to in paragraph 2, for a period of five years, subject, if need be, to Article 24.

Their term of office shall be renewable.

2. The governments of the Member States shall nominate by common accord, after consulting the European Parliament, the person they intend to appoint as President of the Commission.

The governments of the Member States shall, in consultation with the nominee for President, nominate the other persons whom they intend to appoint as members of the Commission.

The President and the other members of the Commission thus nominated shall be subject as a body to a vote of approval by the European Parliament. After approval by the European Parliament, the President and the other members of the Commission shall be appointed by common accord of the governments of the Member States.

3. Paragraphs 1 and 2 shall be applied for the first time to the President and the other members of the Commission whose term of office begins on 7 January 1995.

The President and the other members of the Commission whose term of office begins on 7 January 1993 shall be appointed by common accord of the governments of the Member States. Their term of office shall expire on 6 January 1995.

Article 11

The Commission may appoint a Vice-President or two Vice-Presidents from among its members.

Article 12

Apart from normal replacement, or death, the duties of a member of the Commission shall end when he resigns or is compulsorily retired.

The vacancy thus caused shall be filled for the remainder of the member's term of office by a new member appointed by common accord of the governments of the Member States. The Council may, acting unanimously, decide that such a vacancy need not be filled.

In the event of resignation, compulsory retirement or death, the President shall be replaced for the remainder of his term of office. The procedure laid down in Article 10(2) shall be applicable for the replacement of the President.

Save in the case of compulsory retirement under Article 12a, members of the Commission shall remain in office until they have been replaced.

Article 12a

If any member of the Commission no longer fulfils the conditions required for the performance of his duties or if he has been guilty of serious misconduct, the

Court of Justice may, on application by the Council or the Commission, compulsorily retire him.

Article 13

The Commission shall act by a majority of the number of members provided for in Article 9.

A meeting of the Commission shall be valid only if the number of members laid down in its rules of procedure is present.'

(3) Article 16 shall be replaced by the following:

'Article 16

The Commission shall make all appropriate administrative arrangements for the operation of its departments.

It may set up study committees, including an economic study committee.

The Council and the Commission shall consult each other and shall settle by common accord their methods of cooperation.

The Commission shall adopt its rules of procedure so as to ensure that both it and its departments operate in accordance with the provisions of this Treaty. It shall ensure that these rules are published.'

(4) The following Article shall be inserted:

'Article 17

The Commission shall publish annually, not later than one month before the opening of the session of the European Parliament, a general report on the activities of the Community.'

(5) The following subparagraph shall be added to Article 18:

'The Council shall, acting by a qualified majority, determine any payment to be made instead of remuneration.'

(6) The following Articles shall be inserted:

'Article 20a

The European Parliament may, acting by a majority of its members, request the Commission to submit any appropriate proposal on matters on which it considers that a Community act is required for the purpose of implementing this Treaty.

Article 20b

In the course of its duties, the European Parliament may, at the request of a quarter of its members, set up a temporary Committee of Inquiry to investigate, without prejudice to the powers conferred by this Treaty on other institutions or bodies, alleged contraventions or maladministration in the implementation of Community law, except where the alleged facts are being examined before a court and while the case is still subject to legal proceedings.

The temporary Committee of Inquiry shall cease to exist on the submission of its report.

The detailed provisions governing the exercise of the right of inquiry shall be determined by common accord of the European Parliament, the Council and the Commission.

Article 20c

Any citizen of the Union, and any natural or legal person residing or having its registered office in a Member State, shall have the right to address, individually or in association with other citizens or persons, a petition to the European Parliament on a matter which comes within the Community's fields of activity and which affects him, her or it directly.

Article 20d

1. The European Parliament shall appoint an Ombudsman empowered to receive complaints from any citizen of the Union or any natural or legal person residing or having its registered office in a Member State concerning instances of maladministration in the activities of the Community institutions or bodies, with the exception of the Court of Justice and the Court of First Instance acting in their judicial role.

In accordance with his duties, the Ombudsman shall conduct inquiries for which he finds grounds, either on his own initiative or on the basis of complaints submitted to him direct or through a member of the European Parliament, except where the alleged facts are or have been the subject of legal proceedings. Where the Ombudsman establishes an instance of maladministration, he shall refer the matter to the institution concerned, which shall have a period of three months in which to inform him of its views. The Ombudsman shall then forward a report to the European Parliament and the institution concerned. The person lodging the complaint shall be informed of the outcome of such inquiries.

The Ombudsman shall submit an annual report to the European Parliament on the outcome of his inquiries.

2. The Ombudsman shall be appointed after each election of the European Parliament for the duration of its term of office. The Ombudsman shall be eligible for reappointment.

The Ombudsman may be dismissed by the Court of Justice at the request of the European Parliament if he no longer fulfils the conditions required for the performance of his duties or if he is guilty of serious misconduct.

3. The Ombudsman shall be completely independent in the performance of his duties. In the performance of those duties he shall neither seek nor take instructions from any body. The Ombudsman may not, during his term of office, engage in any other occupation, whether gainful or not.

4. The European Parliament shall, after seeking an opinion from the Commission and with the approval of the Council acting by a qualified majority, lay down the regulations and general conditions governing the performance of the Ombudsman's duties.'

(7) Paragraph 3 of Article 21 shall be replaced by the following:

'3. The European Parliament shall draw up proposals for elections by direct universal suffrage in accordance with a uniform procedure in all Member States.

The Council shall, acting unanimously after obtaining the assent of the European Parliament, which shall act by a majority of its component members, lay down the appropriate provisions, which it shall recommend to Member States for adoption in accordance with their respective constitutional requirements.'

(8) Article 24 shall be replaced by the following:

'Article 24

The European Parliament shall discuss in open session the general report submitted to it by the Commission.

If a motion of censure on the activities of the Commission is tabled before it, the European Parliament shall not vote thereon until at least three days after the motion has been tabled and only by open vote.

If a motion of censure is carried by a two-thirds majority of the votes cast, representing a majority of the members of the European Parliament, the members of the Commission shall resign as a body. They shall continue to deal with current business until they are replaced in accordance with Article 10. In this case, the term of office of the members of the Commission appointed to replace them shall expire on the date on which the term of office of the members of the Commission obliged to resign as a body would have expired.'

(9) The following Articles shall be inserted:

'Article 27

The Council shall consist of a representative of each Member State at ministerial level, authorized to commit the government of that Member State.

The office of President shall be held in turn by each Member State in the Council for a term of six months, in the following order of Member States:

— *for a first cycle of six years: Belgium, Denmark, Germany, Greece, Spain, France, Ireland, Italy, Luxembourg, Netherlands, Portugal, United Kingdom;*

— *for the following cycle of six years: Denmark, Belgium, Greece, Germany, France, Spain, Italy, Ireland, Netherlands, Luxembourg, United Kingdom, Portugal.*

Article 27a

The Council shall meet when convened by its President on his own initiative or at the request of one of its members or of the Commission.'

(10) The following Articles shall be inserted:

'Article 29

The Council shall, acting by a qualified majority, determine the salaries, allowances and pensions of the President and members of the Commission, and of the President, Judges, Advocates-General and Registrar of the Court of Justice. It shall also, again by a qualified majority, determine any payment to be made instead of remuneration.

Article 30

1. A committee consisting of the Permanent Representatives of the Member States shall be responsible for preparing the work of the Council and for carrying out the tasks assigned to it by the Council.

2. The Council shall be assisted by a General Secretariat, under the direction of a Secretary-General. The Secretary-General shall be appointed by the Council acting unanimously.

The Council shall decide on the organization of the General Secretariat.

3. The Council shall adopt its rules of procedure.'

(11) Article 32 shall be replaced by the following:

'Article 32

The Court of Justice shall consist of 13 Judges.

The Court of Justice shall sit in plenary session. It may, however, form Chambers, each consisting of three or five Judges, either to undertake certain preparatory inquiries or to adjudicate on particular categories of cases in accordance with the rules laid down for these purposes.

The Court of Justice shall sit in plenary session when a Member State or a Community institution that is a party to the proceedings so requests.

Should the Court of Justice so request, the Council may, acting unanimously, increase the number of Judges and make the necessary adjustments to the second and third paragraphs of this Article and to the second paragraph of Article 32b.'

(12) Article 32d shall be replaced by the following:

'Article 32d

1. A Court of First Instance shall be attached to the Court of Justice with jurisdiction to hear and determine at first instance, subject to a right of appeal to the Court of Justice on points of law only and in accordance with the conditions laid down by the Statute, certain classes of action or proceeding defined in accordance with the conditions laid down in paragraph 2. The Court of First Instance shall not be competent to hear and determine questions referred for a preliminary ruling under Article 41.

2. At the request of the Court of Justice and after consulting the European Parliament and the Commission, the Council, acting unanimously, shall determine the classes of action or proceeding referred to in paragraph 1, and the composition of the Court of First Instance and shall adopt the necessary adjustments and additional provisions to the Statute of the Court of Justice. Unless the Council decides otherwise, the provisions of this Treaty relating to the Court of Justice, in particular the provisions of the Protocol on the Statute of the Court of Justice, shall apply to the Court of First Instance.

3. The members of the Court of First Instance shall be chosen from persons whose independence is beyond doubt and who possess the ability required for appointment to judicial office; they shall be appointed by common accord of the governments of the Member States for a term of six years. The membership shall be partially renewed every three years. Retiring members shall be eligible for re-appointment.

4. The Court of First Instance shall establish its rules of procedure in agreement with the Court of Justice. Those rules shall require the unanimous approval of the Council.'

(13) Article 33 shall be replaced by the following:

'Article 33

The Court of Justice shall have jurisdiction in actions brought by a Member State or by the Council to have decisions or recommendations of the Commission declared void on grounds of lack of competence, infringement of an essential procedural requirement, infringement of this Treaty or of any rule of law relating to its application, or misuse of powers. The Court of Justice may not, however, examine the evaluation of the situation, resulting from economic facts or circumstances, in the light of which the Commission took its decisions or made its recommendations, save where the Commission is alleged to have misused its powers or to have manifestly failed to observe the provisions of this Treaty or any rule of law relating to its application.

Undertakings or associations referred to in Article 48 may, under the same conditions, institute proceedings against decisions or recommendations concerning them which are individual in character or against general decisions or recommendations which they consider to involve a misuse of powers affecting them.

The proceedings provided for in the first two paragraphs of this Article shall be instituted within one month of the notification or publication, as the case may be, of the decision or recommendation.

The Court of Justice shall have jurisdiction under the same conditions in actions brought by the European Parliament for the purpose of protecting its prerogatives.'

(14) The following chapter shall be inserted:

'CHAPTER V

The Court of Auditors

Article 45a

The Court of Auditors shall carry out the audit.

Article 45b

1. The Court of Auditors shall consist of 12 members.

2. The members of the Court of Auditors shall be chosen from among persons who belong or have belonged in their respective countries to external audit bodies or who are especially qualified for this office. Their independence must be beyond doubt.

3. The members of the Court of Auditors shall be appointed for a term of six years by the Council, acting unanimously after consulting the European Parliament.

However, when the first appointments are made, four members of the Court of Auditors, chosen by lot, shall be appointed for a term of office of four years only.

The members of the Court of Auditors shall be eligible for reappointment.

They shall elect the President of the Court of Auditors from among their number for a term of three years. The President may be re-elected.

4. The members of the Court of Auditors shall, in the general interest of the Community, be completely independent in the performance of their duties.

In the performance of these duties, they shall neither seek nor take instructions from any government or from any other body. They shall refrain from any action incompatible with their duties.

5. The members of the Court of Auditors may not, during their term of office, engage in any other occupation, whether gainful or not. When entering upon their duties they shall give a solemn undertaking that, both during and after their term of office, they will respect the obligations arising therefrom and in particular their duty to behave with integrity and discretion as regards the acceptance, after they have ceased to hold office, of certain appointments or benefits.

6. Apart from normal replacement, or death, the duties of a member of the Court of Auditors shall end when he resigns, or is compulsorily retired by a ruling of the Court of Justice pursuant to paragraph 7.

The vacancy thus caused shall be filled for the remainder of the member's term of office.

Save in the case of compulsory retirement, members of the Court of Auditors shall remain in office until they have been replaced.

7. A member of the Court of Auditors may be deprived of his office or of his right to a pension or other benefits in its stead only if the Court of Justice, at the request of the Court of Auditors, finds that he no longer fulfils the requisite conditions or meets the obligations arising from his office.

8. The Council, acting by a qualified majority, shall determine the conditions of employment of the President and the members of the Court of Auditors and in particular their salaries, allowances and pensions. It shall also, by the same majority, determine any payment to be made instead of remuneration.

9. The provisions of the Protocol on the Privileges and Immunities of the European Communities applicable to the Judges of the Court of Justice shall also apply to the members of the Court of Auditors.

Article 45c

1. The Court of Auditors shall examine the accounts of all revenue and expenditure of the Community. It shall also examine the accounts of all revenue and expenditure of all bodies set up by the Community in so far as the relevant constituent instrument does not preclude such examination.

The Court of Auditors shall provide the European Parliament and the Council with a statement of assurance as to the reliability of the accounts and the legality and regularity of the underlying transactions.

2. The Court of Auditors shall examine whether all revenue referred to in paragraph 1 has been received and all expenditure referred to in that paragraph has been incurred in a lawful and regular manner and whether the financial management has been sound.

The audit of revenue shall be carried out on the basis of the amounts established as due and the amounts actually paid to the Community.

The audit of expenditure shall be carried out on the basis both of commitments undertaken and payments made.

These audits may be carried out before the closure of accounts for the financial year in question.

3. The audit shall be based on records and, if necessary, performed on the spot in the other institutions of the Community and in the Member States. In the Member States the audit shall be carried out in liaison with the national audit bodies or, if these do not have the necessary powers, with the competent national departments. These bodies or departments shall inform the Court of Auditors whether they intend to take part in the audit.

The other institutions of the Community and the national audit bodies or, if these do not have the necessary powers, the competent national departments, shall forward to the Court of Auditors, at its request, any document or information necessary to carry out its task.

4. The Court of Auditors shall draw up an annual report after the close of each financial year. It shall be forwarded to the other institutions of the Community and shall be published, together with the replies of these institutions to the observations of the Court of Auditors, in the Official Journal of the European Communities.

The Court of Auditors may also, at any time, submit observations, particularly in the form of special reports, on specific questions and deliver opinions at the request of one of the other institutions of the Community.

It shall adopt its annual reports, special reports or opinions by a majority of its members.

It shall assist the European Parliament and the Council in exercising their powers of control over the implementation of the budget.

5. The Court of Auditors shall also draw up a separate annual report stating whether the accounting other than that for the expenditure and revenue referred to in paragraph 1 and the financial management by the Commission relating thereto have been effected in a regular manner. It shall draw up this report within six months of the end of the financial year to which the accounts refer and shall submit it to the Commission and the Council. The Commission shall forward it to the European Parliament.'

(15) Article 78c shall be replaced by the following:

'*Article 78c*

The Commission shall implement the administrative budget, in accordance with the provisions of the regulations made pursuant to Article 78h, on its own responsibility and within the limits of the appropriations, having regard to the principles of sound financial management.

The regulations shall lay down detailed rules for each institution concerning its part in effecting its own expenditure.

Within the administrative budget, the Commission may, subject to the limits and conditions laid down in the regulations made pursuant to Article 78h, transfer appropriations from one chapter to another or from one subdivision to another.'

(16) Articles 78e and 78f shall be repealed.

(17) Article 78g shall be replaced by the following:

'Article 78g

1. The European Parliament, acting on a recommendation from the Council, which shall act by a qualified majority, shall give a discharge to the Commission in respect of the implementation of the administrative budget. To this end, the Council and the European Parliament in turn shall examine the accounts and the financial statement referred to in Article 78d, the annual report by the Court of Auditors together with the replies of the institutions under audit to the observations of the Court of Auditors, and any relevant special reports by the Court of Auditors.

2. Before giving a discharge to the Commission, or for any other purpose in connection with the exercise of its powers over the implementation of the administrative budget, the European Parliament may ask to hear the Commission give evidence with regard to the execution of expenditure or the operation of financial control systems. The Commission shall submit any necessary information to the European Parliament at the latter's request.

3. The Commission shall take all appropriate steps to act on the observations in the decisions giving discharge and on other observations by the European Parliament relating to the execution of expenditure, as well as on comments accompanying the recommendations on discharge adopted by the Council.

At the request of the European Parliament or the Council, the Commission shall report on the measures taken in the light of these observations and comments and in particular on the instructions given to the departments which are responsible for the implementation of the administrative budget. These reports shall also be forwarded to the Court of Auditors.'

(18) Article 78h shall be replaced by the following:

'Article 78h

The Council, acting unanimously on a proposal from the Commission and after consulting the European Parliament and obtaining the opinion of the Court of Auditors, shall:

(a) make financial regulations specifying in particular the procedure to be adopted for establishing and implementing the administrative budget and for presenting and auditing accounts;

(b) determine the methods and procedure whereby the budget revenue provided under the arrangements relating to the Communities' own resources shall be made available to the Commission, and determine the measures to be applied, if need be, to meet cash requirements;

(c) lay down rules concerning the responsibility of financial controllers, authorizing officers and accounting officers, and concerning appropriate
arrangements for inspection.'

(19) The following Article shall be inserted:

'*Article 78i*

*Member States shall take the same measures to counter fraud affecting the
financial interests of the Community as they take to counter fraud affecting their
own financial interests.*

*Without prejudice to other provisions of this Treaty, Member States shall coor-
dinate their action aimed at protecting the financial interests of the Community
against fraud. To this end they shall organize, with the help of the Commission,
close and regular cooperation between the competent departments of their administrations.'*

(20) Article 79(a) shall be replaced by the following:

'(a) This Treaty shall not apply to the Faeroe Islands.'

(21) Articles 96 and 98 shall be repealed.

TITLE IV

PROVISIONS AMENDING THE TREATY ESTABLISHING THE EUROPEAN ATOMIC ENERGY COMMUNITY

Article I

The Treaty establishing the European Atomic Energy Community shall be amended in accordance with the provisions of this Article.

(1) Article 3 shall be replaced by the following:

'Article 3

1. The tasks entrusted to the Community shall be carried out by the following institutions:

— *a EUROPEAN PARLIAMENT,*

— *a COUNCIL,*

— *a COMMISSION,*

— *a COURT OF JUSTICE,*

— *a COURT OF AUDITORS.*

Each institution shall act within the limits of the powers conferred upon it by this Treaty.

2. The Council and the Commission shall be assisted by an Economic and Social Committee acting in an advisory capacity.'

(2) The following Articles shall be inserted:

'Article 107a

The European Parliament may, acting by a majority of its members, request the Commission to submit any appropriate proposal on matters on which it considers that a Community act is required for the purpose of implementing this Treaty.

Article 107b

In the course of its duties, the European Parliament may, at the request of a quarter of its members, set up a temporary Committee of Inquiry to investigate, without prejudice to the powers conferred by this Treaty on other institutions or bodies, alleged contraventions or maladministration in the implementation of Community law, except where the alleged facts are being examined before a court and while the case is still subject to legal proceedings.

The temporary Committee of Inquiry shall cease to exist on the submission of its report.

The detailed provisions governing the exercise of the right of inquiry shall be determined by common accord of the European Parliament, the Council and the Commission.

Article 107c

Any citizen of the Union, and any natural or legal person residing or having its registered office in a Member State, shall have the right to address, individually or in association with other citizens or persons, a petition to the European Parliament on a matter which comes within the Community's fields of activity and which affects him, her or it directly.

Article 107d

1. The European Parliament shall appoint an Ombudsman empowered to receive complaints from any citizen of the Union or any natural or legal person residing or having its registered office in a Member State concerning instances of maladministration in the activities of the Community institutions or bodies, with the exception of the Court of Justice and the Court of First Instance acting in their judicial role.

In accordance with his duties, the Ombudsman shall conduct inquiries for which he finds grounds, either on his own initiative or on the basis of complaints submitted to him direct or through a member of the European Parliament, except where the alleged facts are or have been the subject of legal proceedings. Where the Ombudsman establishes an instance of maladministration, he shall refer the matter to the institution concerned, which shall have a period of three months in which to inform him of its views. The Ombudsman shall then forward a report to the European Parliament and the institution concerned. The person lodging the complaint shall be informed of the outcome of such inquiries.

The Ombudsman shall submit an annual report to the European Parliament on the outcome of his inquiries.

2. The Ombudsman shall be appointed after each election of the European Parliament for the duration of its term of office. The Ombudsman shall be eligible for reappointment.

The Ombudsman may be dismissed by the Court of Justice at the request of the European Parliament if he no longer fulfils the conditions required for the performance of his duties or if he is guilty of serious misconduct.

3. The Ombudsman shall be completely independent in the performance of his duties. In the performance of those duties he shall neither seek nor take instructions from any body. The Ombudsman may not, during his term of office, engage in any other occupation, whether gainful or not.

4. The European Parliament shall, after seeking an opinion from the Commission and with the approval of the Council acting by a qualified majority, lay down the regulations and general conditions governing the performance of the Ombudsman's duties.'

(3) Paragraph 3 of Article 108 shall be replaced by the following:

'3. The European Parliament shall draw up proposals for elections by direct universal suffrage in accordance with a uniform procedure in all Member States.

The Council shall, acting unanimously after obtaining the assent of the European Parliament, which shall act by a majority of its component members, lay down the appropriate provisions, which it shall recommend to Member States for adoption in accordance with their respective constitutional requirements.'

(4) The second subparagraph of Article 114 shall be supplemented by the following sentence:

'In this case, the term of office of the members of the Commission appointed to replace them shall expire on the date on which the term of office of the members of the Commission obliged to resign as a body would have expired.'

(5) The following Articles shall be inserted:

'Article 116

The Council shall consist of a representative of each Member State at ministerial level, authorized to commit the government of that Member State.

The office of President shall be held in turn by each Member State in the Council for a term of six months, in the following order of Member States:

— *for a first cycle of six years: Belgium, Denmark, Germany, Greece, Spain, France, Ireland, Italy, Luxembourg, Netherlands, Portugal, United Kingdom;*

— *for the following cycle of six years: Denmark, Belgium, Greece, Germany, France, Spain, Italy, Ireland, Netherlands, Luxembourg, United Kingdom, Portugal.*

Article 117

The Council shall meet when convened by its President on his own initiative or at the request of one of its members or of the Commission.'

(6) The following Article shall be inserted:

'Article 121

1. A committee consisting of the Permanent Representatives of the Member States shall be responsible for preparing the work of the Council and for carrying out the tasks assigned to it by the Council.

2. The Council shall be assisted by a General Secretariat, under the direction of a Secretary-General. The Secretary-General shall be appointed by the Council acting unanimously.

The Council shall decide on the organization of the General Secretariat.

3. The Council shall adopt its rules of procedure.'

(7) The following Article shall be inserted:

'Article 123

The Council shall, acting by a qualified majority, determine the salaries, allowances and pensions of the President and members of the Commission, and of the President, Judges, Advocates-General and Registrar of the Court of Justice. It shall also, again by a qualified majority, determine any payment to be made instead of remuneration.'

(8) The following Articles shall be inserted:

'Article 125

The Commission shall publish annually, not later than one month before the opening of the session of the European Parliament, a general report on the activities of the Community.

Article 126

1. The Commission shall consist of 17 members, who shall be chosen on the grounds of their general competence and whose independence is beyond doubt.

The number of members of the Commission may be altered by the Council, acting unanimously.

Only nationals of the Member States may be members of the Commission.

The Commission must include at least one national of each of the Member States, but may not include more than two members having the nationality of the same State.

2. The members of the Commission shall, in the general interest of the Community, be completely independent in the performance of their duties.

In the performance of these duties, they shall neither seek nor take instructions from any government or from any other body. They shall refrain from any action incompatible with their duties. Each Member State undertakes to respect this principle and not to seek to influence the members of the Commission in the performance of their tasks.

The members of the Commission may not, during their term of office, engage in any other occupation, whether gainful or not. When entering upon their duties they shall give a solemn undertaking that, both during and after their term of office, they will respect the obligations arising therefrom and in particular their duty to behave with integrity and discretion as regards the acceptance, after they have ceased to hold office, of certain appointments or benefits. In the event of any breach of these obligations, the Court of Justice may, on application by the Council or the Commission, rule that the member concerned be, according to the circumstances, either compulsorily retired in accordance with Article 129 or deprived of his right to a pension or other benefits in its stead.

Article 127

1. The members of the Commission shall be appointed, in accordance with the procedure referred to in paragraph 2, for a period of five years, subject, if need be, to Article 114.

Their term of office shall be renewable.

2. The governments of the Member States shall nominate by common accord, after consulting the European Parliament, the person they intend to appoint as President of the Commission.

The governments of the Member States shall, in consultation with the nominee for President, nominate the other persons whom they intend to appoint as members of the Commission.

The President and the other members of the Commission thus nominated shall be subject as a body to a vote of approval by the European Parliament. After approval by the European Parliament, the President and the other members of the Commission shall be appointed by common accord of the governments of the Member States.

3. Paragraphs 1 and 2 shall be applied for the first time to the President and the other members of the Commission whose term of office begins on 7 January 1995.

The President and the other members of the Commission whose term of office begins on 7 January 1993 shall be appointed by common accord of the governments of the Member States. Their term of office shall expire on 6 January 1995.

Article 128

Apart from normal replacement, or death, the duties of a member of the Commission shall end when he resigns or is compulsorily retired.

The vacancy thus caused shall be filled for the remainder of the member's term of office by a new member appointed by common accord of the governments of the Member States. The Council may, acting unanimously, decide that such a vacancy need not be filled.

In the event of resignation, compulsory retirement or death, the President shall be replaced for the remainder of his term of office. The procedure laid down in Article 127(2) shall be applicable for the replacement of the President.

Save in the case of compulsory retirement under Article 129, members of the Commission shall remain in office until they have been replaced.

Article 129

If any member of the Commission no longer fulfils the conditions required for the performance of his duties or if he has been guilty of serious misconduct, the Court of Justice may, on application by the Council or the Commission, compulsorily retire him.

Article 130

The Commission may appoint a Vice-President or two Vice-Presidents from among its members.

Article 131

The Council and the Commission shall consult each other and shall settle by common accord their methods of cooperation.

The Commission shall adopt its rules of procedure so as to ensure that both it and its departments operate in accordance with the provisions of this Treaty. It shall ensure that these rules are published.

Article 132

The Commission shall act by a majority of the number of members provided for in Article 126.

A meeting of the Commission shall be valid only if the number of members laid down in its rules of procedure is present.'

(9) Article 133 shall be repealed.

(10) Article 137 shall be replaced by the following:

'Article 137

The Court of Justice shall consist of 13 Judges.

The Court of Justice shall sit in plenary session. It may, however, form Chambers, each consisting of three or five Judges, either to undertake certain preparatory inquiries or to adjudicate on particular categories of cases in accordance with the rules laid down for these purposes.

The Court of Justice shall sit in plenary session when a Member State or a Community institution that is a party to the proceedings so requests.

Should the Court of Justice so request, the Council may, acting unanimously, increase the number of Judges and make the necessary adjustments to the second and third paragraphs of this Article and to the second paragraph of Article 139.'

(11) Article 140a shall be replaced by the following:

'Article 140a

1. A Court of First Instance shall be attached to the Court of Justice with jurisdiction to hear and determine at first instance, subject to a right of appeal to the Court of Justice on points of law only and in accordance with the conditions laid down by the Statute, certain classes of action or proceeding defined in accordance with the conditions laid down in paragraph 2. The Court of First Instance shall not be competent to hear and determine questions referred for a preliminary ruling under Article 150.

2. At the request of the Court of Justice and after consulting the European Parliament and the Commission, the Council, acting unanimously, shall determine the classes of action or proceeding referred to in paragraph 1 and the composition of the Court of First Instance and shall adopt the necessary adjustments and additional provisions to the Statute of the Court of Justice. Unless the Council decides otherwise, the provisions of this Treaty relating to the Court of Justice, in particular the provisions of the Protocol on the Statute of the Court of Justice, shall apply to the Court of First Instance.

3. The members of the Court of First Instance shall be chosen from persons whose independence is beyond doubt and who possess the ability required for appointment to judicial office; they shall be appointed by common accord of the governments of the Member States for a term of six years. The membership shall be partially renewed every three years. Retiring members shall be eligible for re-appointment.

4. The Court of First Instance shall establish its rules of procedure in agreement with the Court of Justice. Those rules shall require the unanimous approval of the Council.'

(12) Article 143 shall be replaced by the following:

'Article 143

1. If the Court of Justice finds that a Member State has failed to fulfil an obligation under this Treaty, the State shall be required to take the necessary measures to comply with the judgment of the Court of Justice.

2. If the Commission considers that the Member State concerned has not taken such measures it shall, after giving that State the opportunity to submit its observations, issue a reasoned opinion specifying the points on which the Member State concerned has not complied with the judgment of the Court of Justice.

If the Member State concerned fails to take the necessary measures to comply with the Court's judgment within the time-limit laid down by the Commission, the latter may bring the case before the Court of Justice. In so doing it shall specify the amount of the lump sum or penalty payment to be paid by the Member State concerned which it considers appropriate in the circumstances.

If the Court of Justice finds that the Member State concerned has not complied with its judgment it may impose a lump sum or penalty payment on it.

This procedure shall be without prejudice to Article 142.'

(13) Article 146 shall be replaced by the following:

'Article 146

The Court of Justice shall review the legality of acts of the Council and of the Commission, other than recommendations and opinions, and of acts of the European Parliament intended to produce legal effects vis-à-vis *third parties.*

It shall for this purpose have jurisdiction in actions brought by a Member State, the Council or the Commission on grounds of lack of competence, infringement of an essential procedural requirement, infringement of this Treaty or of any rule of law relating to its application, or misuse of powers.

The Court shall have jurisdiction under the same conditions in actions brought by the European Parliament for the purpose of protecting its prerogatives.

Any natural or legal person may, under the same conditions, institute proceedings against a decision addressed to that person or against a decision which, although in the form of a regulation or a decision addressed to another person, is of direct and individual concern to the former.

The proceedings provided for in this Article shall be instituted within two months of the publication of the measure, or of its notification to the plaintiff, or, in the absence thereof, of the day on which it came to the knowledge of the latter, as the case may be.'

(14) The following Section shall be inserted:

'SECTION V

The Court of Auditors

Article 160a

The audit shall be carried out by the Court of Auditors.

Article 160b

1. The Court of Auditors shall consist of 12 members.

2. The members of the Court of Auditors shall be chosen from among persons who belong or have belonged in their respective countries to external audit bodies or who are especially qualified for this office. Their independence must be beyond doubt.

3. The members of the Court of Auditors shall be appointed for a term of six years by the Council, acting unanimously after consulting the European Parliament.

However, when the first appointments are made, four members of the Court of Auditors, chosen by lot, shall be appointed for a term of office of four years only.

The members of the Court of Auditors shall be eligible for reappointment.

They shall elect the President of the Court of Auditors from among their number for a term of three years. The President may be re-elected.

4. The members of the Court of Auditors shall, in the general interest of the Community, be completely independent in the performance of their duties.

In the performance of these duties, they shall neither seek nor take instructions from any government or from any other body. They shall refrain from any action incompatible with their duties.

5. The members of the Court of Auditors may not, during their term of office, engage in any other occupation, whether gainful or not. When entering upon their duties they shall give a solemn undertaking that, both during and after their term of office, they will respect the obligations arising therefrom and in particular their duty to behave with integrity and discretion as regards the acceptance, after they have ceased to hold office, of certain appointments or benefits.

6. Apart from normal replacement, or death, the duties of a member of the Court of Auditors shall end when he resigns, or is compulsorily retired by a ruling of the Court of Justice pursuant to paragraph 7.

The vacancy thus caused shall be filled for the remainder of the member's term of office.

Save in the case of compulsory retirement, members of the Court of Auditors shall remain in office until they have been replaced.

7. A member of the Court of Auditors may be deprived of his office or of his right to a pension or other benefits in its stead only if the Court of Justice, at the request of the Court of Auditors, finds that he no longer fulfils the requisite conditions or meets the obligations arising from his office.

8. The Council, acting by a qualified majority, shall determine the conditions of employment of the President and the members of the Court of Auditors and in particular their salaries, allowances and pensions. It shall also, by the same majority, determine any payment to be made instead of remuneration.

9. The provisions of the Protocol on the Privileges and Immunities of the European Communities applicable to the Judges of the Court of Justice shall also apply to the members of the Court of Auditors.

Article 160c

1. The Court of Auditors shall examine the accounts of all revenue and expenditure of the Community. It shall also examine the accounts of all revenue and expenditure of all bodies set up by the Community in so far as the relevant constituent instrument does not preclude such examination.

The Court of Auditors shall provide the European Parliament and the Council with a statement of assurance as to the reliability of the accounts and the legality and regularity of the underlying transactions.

2. *The Court of Auditors shall examine whether all revenue has been received and all expenditure incurred in a lawful and regular manner and whether the financial management has been sound.*

The audit of revenue shall be carried out on the basis of the amounts established as due and the amounts actually paid to the Community.

The audit of expenditure shall be carried out on the basis both of commitments undertaken and payments made.

These audits may be carried out before the closure of accounts for the financial year in question.

3. *The audit shall be based on records and, if necessary, performed on the spot in the other institutions of the Community and in the Member States. In the Member States the audit shall be carried out in liaison with the national audit bodies or, if these do not have the necessary powers, with the competent national departments. These bodies or departments shall inform the Court of Auditors whether they intend to take part in the audit.*

The other institutions of the Community and the national audit bodies or, if these do not have the necessary powers, the competent national department, shall forward to the Court of Auditors, at its request, any document or information necessary to carry out its task.

4. *The Court of Auditors shall draw up an annual report after the close of each financial year. It shall be forwarded to the other institutions of the Community and shall be published, together with the replies of these institutions to the observations of the Court of Auditors, in the* Official Journal of the European Communities.

The Court of Auditors may also, at any time, submit observations, particularly in the form of special reports, on specific questions and deliver opinions at the request of one of the other institutions of the Community.

It shall adopt its annual reports, special reports or opinions by a majority of its members.

It shall assist the European Parliament and the Council in exercising their powers of control over the implementation of the budget.'

(15) Article 166 shall be replaced by the following:

'Article 166

The number of members of the Economic and Social Committee shall be as follows:

Belgium	*12*
Denmark	*9*
Germany	*24*
Greece	*12*
Spain	*21*
France	*24*
Ireland	*9*
Italy	*24*
Luxembourg	*6*
Netherlands	*12*
Portugal	*12*
United Kingdom	*24*

The members of the Committee shall be appointed by the Council, acting unanimously, for four years. Their appointments shall be renewable.

The members of the Committee may not be bound by any mandatory instructions. They shall be completely independent in the performance of their duties, in the general interest of the Community.

The Council, acting by a qualified majority, shall determine the allowances of members of the Committee.'

(16) Article 168 shall be replaced by the following:

'Article 168

The Committee shall elect its chairman and officers from among its members for a term of two years.

It shall adopt its rules of procedure.

The Committee shall be convened by its chairman at the request of the Council or of the Commission. It may also meet on its own initiative.'

(17) Article 170 shall be replaced by the following:

'Article 170

The Committee must be consulted by the Council or by the Commission where this Treaty so provides. The Committee may be consulted by these institutions in all cases in which they consider it appropriate. It may issue an opinion on its own initiative in cases in which it considers such action appropriate.

The Council or the Commission shall, if it considers it necessary, set the Committee, for the submission of its opinion, a time-limit which may not be less than one month from the date on which the chairman receives notification to this effect. Upon expiry of the time-limit, the absence of an opinion shall not prevent further action.

The opinion of the Committee and that of the specialized section, together with a record of the proceedings, shall be forwarded to the Council and to the Commission.'

(18) Paragraphs 1 to 3 of Article 172 shall be repealed.

(19) Article 173 shall be replaced by the following:

'Article 173

Without prejudice to other revenue, the budget shall be financed wholly from own resources.

The Council, acting unanimously on a proposal from the Commission and after consulting the European Parliament, shall lay down provisions relating to the system of own resources of the Community, which it shall recommend to the Member States for adoption in accordance with their respective constitutional requirements.'

(20) The following Article shall be inserted:

'Article 173a

With a view to maintaining budgetary discipline, the Commission shall not make any proposal for a Community act, or alter its proposals, or adopt any implementing measure which is likely to have appreciable implications for the budget without providing the assurance that that proposal or that measure is capable of being financed within the limit of the Community's own resources arising under provisions laid down by the Council pursuant to Article 173.'

(21) Article 179 shall be replaced by the following:

'Article 179

The Commission shall implement the budgets, in accordance with the provisions of the regulations made pursuant to Article 183, on its own responsibility and within the limits of the appropriations, having regard to the principles of sound financial management.

The regulations shall lay down detailed rules for each institution concerning its part in effecting its own expenditure.

Within the budgets, the Commission may, subject to the limits and conditions laid down in the regulations made pursuant to Article 183, transfer appropriations from one chapter to another or from one subdivision to another.'

(22) Articles 180 and 180a shall be repealed.

(23) Article 180b shall be replaced by the following:

'Article 180b

1. The European Parliament, acting on a recommendation from the Council which shall act by a qualified majority, shall give a discharge to the Commission in respect of the implementation of the budget. To this end, the Council and the European Parliament in turn shall examine the accounts and the financial statement referred to in Article 179a, the annual report by the Court of Auditors together with the replies of the institutions under audit to the observations of the Court of Auditors, and any relevant special reports by the Court of Auditors.

2. Before giving a discharge to the Commission, or for any other purpose in connection with the exercise of its powers over the implementation of the budget, the European Parliament may ask to hear the Commission give evidence with regard to the execution of expenditure or the operation of financial control systems. The Commission shall submit any necessary information to the European Parliament at the latter's request.

3. The Commission shall take all appropriate steps to act on the observations in the decisions giving discharge and on other observations by the European Parliament relating to the execution of expenditure, as well as on comments accompanying the recommendations on discharge adopted by the Council.

At the request of the European Parliament or the Council, the Commission shall report on the measures taken in the light of these observations and comments and in particular on the instructions given to the departments which are responsible for the implementation of the budgets. These reports shall also be forwarded to the Court of Auditors.'

(24) Article 183 shall be replaced by the following:

'Article 183

The Council, acting unanimously on a proposal from the Commission and after consulting the European Parliament and obtaining the opinion of the Court of Auditors, shall:

(a) make financial regulations specifying in particular the procedure to be adopted for establishing and implementing the budget and for presenting and auditing accounts;

(b) determine the methods and procedure whereby the budget revenue provided under the arrangements relating to the Community's own resources shall be made available to the Commission, and determine the measures to be applied, if need be, to meet cash requirements;

(c) lay down rules concerning the responsibility of financial controllers, authorizing officers and accounting officers, and concerning appropriate arrangements for inspection.'

(25) The following Article shall be inserted:

'Article 183a

Member States shall take the same measures to counter fraud affecting the financial interests of the Community as they take to counter fraud affecting their own financial interests.

Without prejudice to other provisions of this Treaty, Member States shall coordinate their actions aimed at protecting the financial interests of the Community against fraud. To this end they shall organize, with the help of the Commission, close and regular cooperation between the competent departments of their administrations.'

(26) Article 198(a) shall be replaced by the following:

'(a) This Treaty shall not apply to the Faeroe Islands.'

(27) Article 201 shall be replaced by the following:

'Article 201

The Community shall establish close cooperation with the Organization for Economic Cooperation and Development, the details of which shall be determined by common accord.'

(28) Articles 204 and 205 shall be repealed.

(29) Article 206 shall be replaced by the following:

'Article 206

The Community may conclude with one or more States or international organizations agreements establishing an association involving reciprocal rights and obligations, common action and special procedures.

These agreements shall be concluded by the Council, acting unanimously after consulting the European Parliament.

Where such agreements call for amendments to this Treaty, these amendments shall first be adopted in accordance with the procedure laid down in Article N of the Treaty on European Union.'

TITLE V

PROVISIONS ON A COMMON FOREIGN AND SECURITY POLICY

Article J

A common foreign and security policy is hereby established which shall be governed by the following provisions.

Article J.1

1. The Union and its Member States shall define and implement a common foreign and security policy, governed by the provisions of this Title and covering all areas of foreign and security policy.

2. The objectives of the common foreign and security policy shall be:

— to safeguard the common values, fundamental interests and independence of the Union;

— to strengthen the security of the Union and its Member States in all ways;

— to preserve peace and strengthen international security, in accordance with the principles of the United Nations Charter as well as the principles of the Helsinki Final Act and the objectives of the Paris Charter;

— to promote international cooperation;

— to develop and consolidate democracy and the rule of law, and respect for human rights and fundamental freedoms.

3. The Union shall pursue these objectives:

— by establishing systematic cooperation between Member States in the conduct of policy, in accordance with Article J.2;

— by gradually implementing, in accordance with Article J.3, joint action in the areas in which the Member States have important interests in common.

4. The Member States shall support the Union's external and security policy actively and unreservedly in a spirit of loyalty and mutual solidarity. They shall refrain from any action which is contrary to the interests of the Union or likely to impair its effectiveness as a cohesive force in international relations. The Council shall ensure that these principles are complied with.

Article J.2

1. Member States shall inform and consult one another within the Council on any matter of foreign and security policy of general interest in order to ensure that their combined influence is exerted as effectively as possible by means of concerted and convergent action.

2. Whenever it deems it necessary, the Council shall define a common position.

Member States shall ensure that their national policies conform to the common positions.

3. Member States shall coordinate their action in international organizations and at international conferences. They shall uphold the common positions in such forums.

In international organizations and at international conferences where not all the Member States participate, those which do take part shall uphold the common positions.

Article J.3

The procedure for adopting joint action in matters covered by the foreign and security policy shall be the following:

1. The Council shall decide, on the basis of general guidelines from the European Council, that a matter should be the subject of joint action.

   Whenever the Council decides on the principle of joint action, it shall lay down the specific scope, the Union's general and specific objectives in carrying out such action, if necessary its duration, and the means, procedures and conditions for its implementation.

2. The Council shall, when adopting the joint action and at any stage during its development, define those matters on which decisions are to be taken by a qualified majority.

   Where the Council is required to act by a qualified majority pursuant to the preceding subparagraph, the votes of its members shall be weighted in accordance with Article 148(2) of the Treaty establishing the European Community, and for their adoption, acts of the Council shall require at least 54 votes in favour, cast by at least eight members.

3. If there is a change in circumstances having a substantial effect on a question subject to joint action, the Council shall review the principles and objectives of that action and take the necessary decisions. As long as the Council has not acted, the joint action shall stand.

4. Joint actions shall commit the Member States in the positions they adopt and in the conduct of their activity.

5. Whenever there is any plan to adopt a national position or take national action pursuant to a joint action, information shall be provided in time to allow, if necessary, for prior consultations within the Council. The obligation to provide prior information shall not apply to measures which are merely a national transposition of Council decisions.

6. In cases of imperative need arising from changes in the situation and failing a Council decision, Member States may take the necessary measures as a matter of urgency having regard to the general objectives of the joint action. The Member State concerned shall inform the Council immediately of any such measures.

7. Should there be any major difficulties in implementing a joint action, a Member State shall refer them to the Council which shall discuss them and seek appropriate solutions. Such solutions shall not run counter to the objectives of the joint action or impair its effectiveness.

Article J.4

1. The common foreign and security policy shall include all questions related to the security of the Union, including the eventual framing of a common defence policy, which might in time lead to a common defence.

2. The Union requests the Western European Union (WEU), which is an integral part of the development of the Union, to elaborate and implement decisions and actions of the Union which have defence implications. The Council shall, in agreement with the institutions of the WEU, adopt the necessary practical arrangements.

3. Issues having defence implications dealt with under this Article shall not be subject to the procedures set out in Article J.3.

4. The policy of the Union in accordance with this Article shall not prejudice the specific character of the security and defence policy of certain Member States and shall respect the obligations of certain Member States under the North Atlantic Treaty and be compatible with the common security and defence policy established within that framework.

5. The provisions of this Article shall not prevent the development of closer cooperation between two or more Member States on a bilateral level, in the framework of the WEU and the Atlantic Alliance, provided such cooperation does not run counter to or impede that provided for in this Title.

6. With a view to furthering the objective of this Treaty, and having in view the date of 1998 in the context of Article XII of the Brussels Treaty, the provisions of this Article may be revised as provided for in Article N(2) on the basis of a report to be presented in 1996 by the Council to the European Council, which shall include an evaluation of the progress made and the experience gained until then.

Article J.5

1. The Presidency shall represent the Union in matters coming within the common foreign and security policy.

2. The Presidency shall be responsible for the implementation of common measures; in that capacity it shall in principle express the position of the Union in international organizations and international conferences.

3. In the tasks referred to in paragraphs 1 and 2, the Presidency shall be assisted if need be by the previous and next Member States to hold the Presidency. The Commission shall be fully associated in these tasks.

4. Without prejudice to Article J.2(3) and Article J.3(4), Member States represented in international organizations or international conferences where not all the Member States participate shall keep the latter informed of any matter of common interest.

Member States which are also members of the United Nations Security Council will concert and keep the other Member States fully informed. Member States which are permanent members of the Security Council will, in the execution of their functions, ensure the defence of the positions and the interests of the Union, without prejudice to their responsibilities under the provisions of the United Nations Charter.

Article J.6

The diplomatic and consular missions of the Member States and the Commission Delegations in third countries and international conferences, and their representations to international organizations, shall cooperate in ensuring that the common positions and common measures adopted by the Council are complied with and implemented.

They shall step up cooperation by exchanging information, carrying out joint assessments and contributing to the implementation of the provisions referred to in Article 8c of the Treaty establishing the European Community.

Article J.7

The Presidency shall consult the European Parliament on the main aspects and the basic choices of the common foreign and security policy and shall ensure that the views of the European Parliament are duly taken into consideration. The European Parliament shall be kept regularly informed by the Presidency and the Commission of the development of the Union's foreign and security policy.

The European Parliament may ask questions of the Council or make recommendations to it. It shall hold an annual debate on progress in implementing the common foreign and security policy.

Article J.8

1. The European Council shall define the principles of and general guidelines for the common foreign and security policy.

2. The Council shall take the decisions necessary for defining and implementing the common foreign and security policy on the basis of the general guidelines adopted by the European Council. It shall ensure the unity, consistency and effectiveness of action by the Union.

The Council shall act unanimously, except for procedural questions and in the case referred to in Article J.3(2).

3. Any Member State or the Commission may refer to the Council any question relating to the common foreign and security policy and may submit proposals to the Council.

4. In cases requiring a rapid decision, the Presidency, of its own motion, or at the request of the Commission or a Member State, shall convene an extraordinary Council meeting within 48 hours or, in an emergency, within a shorter period.

5. Without prejudice to Article 151 of the Treaty establishing the European Community, a Political Committee consisting of Political Directors shall monitor the international situation in the areas covered by common foreign and security policy and contribute to the definition of policies by delivering opinions to the Council at the request of the Council or on its own initiative. It shall also monitor the implementation of agreed policies, without prejudice to the responsibility of the Presidency and the Commission.

Article J.9

The Commission shall be fully associated with the work carried out in the common foreign and security policy field.

Article J.10

On the occasion of any review of the security provisions under Article J.4, the Conference which is convened to that effect shall also examine whether any other amendments need to be made to provisions relating to the common foreign and security policy.

Article J.11

1. The provisions referred to in Articles 137, 138, 139 to 142, 146, 147, 150 to 153, 157 to 163 and 217 of the Treaty establishing the European Community shall apply to the provisions relating to the areas referred to in this Title.

2. Administrative expenditure which the provisions relating to the areas referred to in this Title entail for the institutions shall be charged to the budget of the European Communities.

The Council may also:

— either decide unanimously that operational expenditure to which the implementation of those provisions gives rise is to be charged to the budget of the European Communities; in that event, the budgetary procedure laid down in the Treaty establishing the European Community shall be applicable;

— or determine that such expenditure shall be charged to the Member States, where appropriate in accordance with a scale to be decided.

TITLE VI

PROVISIONS ON COOPERATION IN THE FIELDS OF JUSTICE AND HOME AFFAIRS

Article K

Cooperation in the fields of justice and home affairs shall be governed by the following provisions.

Article K.1

For the purposes of achieving the objectives of the Union, in particular the free movement of persons, and without prejudice to the powers of the European Community, Member States shall regard the following areas as matters of common interest:

(1) asylum policy;

(2) rules governing the crossing by persons of the external borders of the Member States and the exercise of controls thereon;

(3) immigration policy and policy regarding nationals of third countries:

    (a) conditions of entry and movement by nationals of third countries on the territory of Member States;

    (b) conditions of residence by nationals of third countries on the territory of Member States, including family reunion and access to employment;

(c) combating unauthorized immigration, residence and work by nationals of third countries on the territory of Member States;

(4) combating drug addiction in so far as this is not covered by (7) to (9);

(5) combating fraud on an international scale in so far as this is not covered by 7 to 9;

(6) judicial cooperation in civil matters;

(7) judicial cooperation in criminal matters;

(8) customs cooperation;

(9) police cooperation for the purposes of preventing and combating terrorism, unlawful drug trafficking and other serious forms of international crime, including if necessary certain aspects of customs cooperation, in connection with the organization of a Union-wide system for exchanging information within a European Police Office (Europol).

Article K.2

1. The matters referred to in Article K.1 shall be dealt with in compliance with the European Convention for the Protection of Human Rights and Fundamental Freedoms of 4 November 1950 and the Convention relating to the Status of Refugees of 28 July 1951 and having regard to the protection afforded by Member States to persons persecuted on political grounds.

2. This Title shall not affect the exercise of the responsibilities incumbent upon Member States with regard to the maintenance of law and order and the safeguarding of internal security.

Article K.3

1. In the areas referred to in Article K.1, Member States shall inform and consult one another within the Council with a view to coordinating their action. To that end, they shall establish collaboration between the relevant departments of their administrations.

2. The Council may:

— on the initiative of any Member State or of the Commission, in the areas referred to in Article K.1(1) to (6);

— on the initiative of any Member State, in the areas referred to in Article K.1(7) to (9):

    (a) adopt joint positions and promote, using the appropriate form and procedures, any cooperation contributing to the pursuit of the objectives of the Union;

    (b) adopt joint action in so far as the objectives of the Union can be attained better by joint action than by the Member States acting individually on account of the scale or effects of the action envisaged; it may decide that measures implementing joint action are to be adopted by a qualified majority;

    (c) without prejudice to Article 220 of the Treaty establishing the European Community, draw up conventions which it shall recommend to the Member States for adoption in accordance with their respective constitutional requirements.

    Unless otherwise provided by such conventions, measures implementing them shall be adopted within the Council by a majority of two-thirds of the High Contracting Parties.

    Such conventions may stipulate that the Court of Justice shall have jurisdiction to interpret their provisions and to rule on any disputes regarding their application, in accordance with such arrangements as they may lay down.

Article K.4

1. A Coordinating Committee shall be set up consisting of senior officials. In addition to its coordinating role, it shall be the task of the Committee to:

— give opinions for the attention of the Council, either at the Council's request or on its own initiative;

— contribute, without prejudice to Article 151 of the Treaty establishing the European Community, to the preparation of the Council's discussions in the areas referred to in Article K.1 and, in accordance with the conditions laid down in Article 100d of the Treaty establishing the European Community, in the areas referred to in Article 100c of that Treaty.

2. The Commission shall be fully associated with the work in the areas referred to in this Title.

3. The Council shall act unanimously, except on matters of procedure and in cases where Article K.3 expressly provides for other voting rules.

Where the Council is required to act by a qualified majority, the votes of its members shall be weighted as laid down in Article 148(2) of the Treaty establishing the European Community, and for their adoption, acts of the Council shall require at least 54 votes in favour, cast by at least eight members.

Article K.5

Within international organizations and at international conferences in which they take part, Member States shall defend the common positions adopted under the provisions of this Title.

Article K.6

The Presidency and the Commission shall regularly inform the European Parliament of discussions in the areas covered by this Title.

The Presidency shall consult the European Parliament on the principal aspects of activities in the areas referred to in this Title and shall ensure that the views of the European Parliament are duly taken into consideration.

The European Parliament may ask questions of the Council or make recommendations to it. Each year, it shall hold a debate on the progress made in implementation of the areas referred to in this Title.

Article K.7

The provisions of this Title shall not prevent the establishment or development of closer cooperation between two or more Member States in so far as such cooperation does not conflict with, or impede, that provided for in this Title.

Article K.8

1. The provisions referred to in Articles 137, 138, 139 to 142, 146, 147, 150 to 153, 157 to 163 and 217 of the Treaty establishing the European Community shall apply to the provisions relating to the areas referred to in this Title.

2. Administrative expenditure which the provisions relating to the areas referred to in this Title entail for the institutions shall be charged to the budget of the European Communities.

The Council may also:

— either decide unanimously that operational expenditure to which the implementation of those provisions gives rise is to be charged to the budget of the European Communities; in that event, the budgetary procedure laid down in the Treaty establishing the European Community shall be applicable;

— or determine that such expenditure shall be charged to the Member States, where appropriate in accordance with a scale to be decided.

Article K.9

The Council, acting unanimously on the initiative of the Commission or a Member State, may decide to apply Article 100c of the Treaty establishing the European Community to action in areas referred to in Article K.1(1) to (6), and at the same time determine the relevant voting conditions relating to it. It shall recommend the Member States to adopt that decision in accordance with their respective constitutional requirements.

TITLE VII

FINAL PROVISIONS

Article L

The provisions of the Treaty establishing the European Community, the Treaty establishing the European Coal and Steel Community and the Treaty establishing the European Atomic Energy Community concerning the powers of the Court of Justice of the European Communities and the exercise of those powers shall apply only to the following provisions of this Treaty:

(a) provisions amending the Treaty establishing the European Economic Community with a view to establishing the European Community, the Treaty establishing the European Coal and Steel Community and the Treaty establishing the European Atomic Energy Community;

(b) the third subparagraph of Article K.3(2)(c);

(c) Articles L to S.

Article M

Subject to the provisions amending the Treaty establishing the European Economic Community with a view to establishing the European Community, the Treaty establishing the European Coal and Steel Community and the Treaty establishing the European Atomic Energy Community, and to these final provisions, nothing in this Treaty shall affect the Treaties establishing the European Communities or the subsequent Treaties and Acts modifying or supplementing them.

Article N

1. The government of any Member State or the Commission may submit to the Council proposals for the amendment of the Treaties on which the Union is founded.

If the Council, after consulting the European Parliament and, where appropriate, the Commission, delivers an opinion in favour of calling a conference of representatives of the governments of the Member States, the conference shall be convened by the President of the Council for the purpose of determining by common accord the amendments to be made to those Treaties. The European Central Bank shall also be consulted in the case of institutional changes in the monetary area.

The amendments shall enter into force after being ratified by all the Member States in accordance with their respective constitutional requirements.

2. A conference of representatives of the governments of the Member States shall be convened in 1996 to examine those provisions of this Treaty for which revision is provided, in accordance with the objectives set out in Articles A and B.

Article O

Any European State may apply to become a Member of the Union. It shall address its application to the Council, which shall act unanimously after consulting the Commission and after receiving the assent of the European Parliament, which shall act by an absolute majority of its component members.

The conditions of admission and the adjustments to the Treaties on which the Union is founded which such admission entails shall be the subject of an agreement between the Member States and the applicant State. This agreement shall be submitted for ratification by all the contracting States in accordance with their respective constitutional requirements.

Article P

1. Articles 2 to 7 and 10 to 19 of the Treaty establishing a Single Council and a Single Commission of the European Communities, signed in Brussels on 8 April 1965, are hereby repealed.

2. Article 2, Article 3(2) and Title III of the Single European Act signed in Luxembourg on 17 February 1986 and in The Hague on 28 February 1986 are hereby repealed.

Article Q

This Treaty is concluded for an unlimited period.

Article R

1. This Treaty shall be ratified by the High Contracting Parties in accordance with their respective constitutional requirements. The instruments of ratification shall be deposited with the government of the Italian Republic.

2. This Treaty shall enter into force on 1 January 1993, provided that all the instruments of ratification have been deposited, or, failing that, on the first day of the month following the deposit of the instrument of ratification by the last signatory State to take this step.

Article S

This Treaty, drawn up in a single original in the Danish, Dutch, English, French, German, Greek, Irish, Italian, Portuguese and Spanish languages, the texts in each of these languages being equally authentic, shall be deposited in the archives of the government of the Italian Republic, which will transmit a certified copy to each of the governments of the other signatory States.

EN FE DE LO CUAL, los plenipotenciarios abajo firmantes suscriben el presente Tratado.

TIL BEKRÆFTELSE HERAF har undertegnede befuldmægtigede underskrevet denne Traktat.

ZU URKUND DESSEN haben die unterzeichneten Bevollmächtigten ihre Unterschriften unter diesen Vertrag gesetzt.

ΕΙΣ ΠΙΣΤΩΣΗ ΤΩΝ ΑΝΩΤΕΡΩ, οι υπογεγραμμένοι πληρεξούσιοι υπέγραψαν την παρούσα συνθήκη.

IN WITNESS WHEREOF the undersigned Plenipotentiaries have signed this Treaty.

EN FOI DE QUOI, les plénipotentiaires soussignés ont apposé leurs signatures au bas du présent traité.

DÁ FHIANÚ SIN, chuir na Lánchumhachtaigh thíos-sínithe a lámh leis an gConradh seo.

IN FEDE DI CHE, i plenipotenziari sottoscritti hanno apposto le loro firme in calce al presente trattato.

TEN BLIJKE WAARVAN de ondergetekende gevolmachtigden hun handtekening onder dit Verdrag hebben gesteld.

EM FÉ DO QUE, os plenipotenciários abaixo assinados apuseram as suas assinaturas no final do presente Tratado.

Hecho en Maastricht, el siete de febrero de mil novecientos noventa y dos.

Udfærdiget i Maastricht, den syvende februar nitten hundrede og tooghalvfems.

Geschehen zu Maastricht am siebten Februar neunzehnhundertzweiundneunzig.

Έγινε στο Μάαστριχτ, στις εφτά Φεβρουαρίου χίλια εννιακόσια ενενήντα δύο.

Done at Maastricht on the seventh day of February in the year one thousand nine hundred and ninety-two.

Fait à Maastricht, le sept février mil neuf cent quatre-vingt-douze.

Arna dhéanamh i Maastricht, an seachtú lá d'Fheabhra, míle naoi gcéad nócha a dó.

Fatto a Maastricht, addì sette febbraio millenovecentonovantadue.

Gedaan te Maastricht, de zevende februari negentienhonderd twee-en-negentig.

Feito em Maastricht, em sete de Fevereiro de mil novecentos e noventa e dois.

Pour Sa Majesté le Roi des Belges
Voor Zijne Majesteit de Koning der Belgen

For Hendes Majestæt Danmarks Dronning

Für den Präsidenten der Bundesrepublik Deutschland

Για τον Πρόεδρο της Ελληνικής Δημοκρατίας

Por Su Majestad el Rey de España

Pour le Président de la République française

Thar ceann Uachtarán na hEireann
For the President of Ireland

Per il Presidente della Repubblica italiana

Pour Son Altesse Royale le Grand-Duc de Luxembourg

Voor Hare Majesteit de Koningin der Nederlanden

Pelo Presidente da República Portuguesa

For Her Majesty the Queen of the United Kingdom of Great Britain and
Northern Ireland

PROTOCOLS

PROTOCOL

ON THE ACQUISITION OF PROPERTY IN DENMARK

THE HIGH CONTRACTING PARTIES,

DESIRING to settle certain particular problems relating to Denmark,

HAVE AGREED upon the following provision, which shall be annexed to the Treaty establishing the European Community:

Notwithstanding the provisions of this Treaty, Denmark may maintain the existing legislation on the acquisition of second homes.

PROTOCOL

CONCERNING ARTICLE 119 OF THE TREATY ESTABLISHING THE EUROPEAN COMMUNITY

THE HIGH CONTRACTING PARTIES,

HAVE AGREED upon the following provision, which shall be annexed to the Treaty establishing the European Community:

For the purposes of Article 119 of this Treaty, benefits under occupational social security schemes shall not be considered as remuneration if and in so far as they are attributable to periods of employment prior to 17 May 1990, except in the case of workers or those claiming under them who have before that date initiated legal proceedings or introduced an equivalent claim under the applicable national law.

PROTOCOL

ON THE STATUTE OF THE EUROPEAN SYSTEM OF CENTRAL BANKS AND OF THE EUROPEAN CENTRAL BANK

THE HIGH CONTRACTING PARTIES,

DESIRING to lay down the Statute of the European System of Central Banks and of the European Central Bank provided for in Article 4a of the Treaty establishing the European Community,

HAVE AGREED upon the following provisions, which shall be annexed to the Treaty establishing the European Community:

CHAPTER I

CONSTITUTION OF THE ESCB

Article 1

The European System of Central Banks

1.1. The European System of Central Banks (ESCB) and the European Central Bank (ECB) shall be established in accordance with Article 4a of this Treaty; they shall perform their tasks and carry on their activities in accordance with the provisions of this Treaty and of this Statute.

1.2. In accordance with Article 106(1) of this Treaty, the ESCB shall be composed of the ECB and of the central banks of the Member States ('national central banks'). The Institut monétaire luxembourgeois will be the central bank of Luxembourg.

CHAPTER II

OBJECTIVES AND TASKS OF THE ESCB

Article 2

Objectives

In accordance with Article 105(1) of this Treaty, the primary objective of the ESCB shall be to maintain price stability. Without prejudice to the objective of price stability, it shall support the general economic policies in the Community with a view to contributing to the achievement of the objectives of the Community as laid down in Article 2 of this Treaty. The ESCB shall act in accordance with the principle of an open market economy with free competition, favouring an efficient allocation of resources, and in compliance with the principles set out in Article 3a of this Treaty.

Article 3

Tasks

3.1. In accordance with Article 105(2) of this Treaty, the basic tasks to be carried out through the ESCB shall be:

— to define and implement the monetary policy of the Community;

— to conduct foreign-exchange operations consistent with the provisions of Article 109 of this Treaty;

— to hold and manage the official foreign reserves of the Member States;

— to promote the smooth operation of payment systems.

3.2. In accordance with Article 105(3) of this Treaty, the third indent of Article 3.1 shall be without prejudice to the holding and management by the governments of Member States of foreign-exchange working balances.

3.3. In accordance with Article 105(5) of this Treaty, the ESCB shall contribute to the smooth conduct of policies pursued by the competent authorities relating to the prudential supervision of credit institutions and the stability of the financial system.

Article 4

Advisory functions

In accordance with Article 105(4) of this Treaty:

(a) the ECB shall be consulted:

— on any proposed Community act in its fields of competence;

— by national authorities regarding any draft legislative provision in its fields of competence, but within the limits and under the conditions set out by the Council in accordance with the procedure laid down in Article 42;

(b) the ECB may submit opinions to the appropriate Community institutions or bodies or to national authorities on matters in its fields of competence.

Article 5

Collection of statistical information

5.1. In order to undertake the tasks of the ESCB, the ECB, assisted by the national central banks, shall collect the necessary statistical information either from the competent national authorities or directly from economic agents. For these purposes it shall cooperate with the Community institutions or bodies and with the competent authorities of the Member States or third countries and with international organizations.

5.2. The national central banks shall carry out, to the extent possible, the tasks described in Article 5.1.

5.3. The ECB shall contribute to the harmonization, where necessary, of the rules and practices governing the collection, compilation and distribution of statistics in the areas within its fields of competence.

5.4. The Council, in accordance with the procedure laid down in Article 42, shall define the natural and legal persons subject to reporting requirements, the confidentiality regime and the appropriate provisions for enforcement.

Article 6

International cooperation

6.1. In the field of international cooperation involving the tasks entrusted to the ESCB, the ECB shall decide how the ESCB shall be represented.

6.2. The ECB and, subject to its approval, the national central banks may participate in international monetary institutions.

6.3. Articles 6.1 and 6.2 shall be without prejudice to Article 109(4) of this Treaty.

CHAPTER III

ORGANIZATION OF THE ESCB

Article 7

Independence

In accordance with Article 107 of this Treaty, when exercising the powers and carrying out the tasks and duties conferred upon them by this Treaty and this Statute, neither the ECB, nor a national central bank, nor any member of their decision-making bodies shall seek or take instructions from Community institutions or bodies, from any government of a Member State or from any other body. The Community institutions and bodies and the governments of the Member States undertake to respect this principle and not to seek to influence the members of the decision-making bodies of the ECB or of the national central banks in the performance of their tasks.

Article 8

General principle

The ESCB shall be governed by the decision-making bodies of the ECB.

Article 9

The European Central Bank

9.1. The ECB which, in accordance with Article 106(2) of this Treaty, shall have legal personality, shall enjoy in each of the Member States the most extensive legal capacity accorded to legal persons under its law; it may, in particular, acquire or dispose of movable and immovable property and may be a party to legal proceedings.

9.2. The ECB shall ensure that the tasks conferred upon the ESCB under Article 105(2), (3) and (5) of this Treaty are implemented either by its own activities pursuant to this Statute or through the national central banks pursuant to Articles 12.1 and 14.

9.3. In accordance with Article 106(3) of this Treaty, the decision-making bodies of the ECB shall be the Governing Council and the Executive Board.

Article 10

The Governing Council

10.1. In accordance with Article 109a(1) of this Treaty, the Governing Council shall comprise the members of the Executive Board of the ECB and the Governors of the national central banks.

10.2. Subject to Article 10.3, only members of the Governing Council present in person shall have the right to vote. By way of derogation from this rule, the Rules of Procedure referred to in Article 12.3 may lay down that members of the Governing Council may cast their vote by means of teleconferencing. These rules shall also provide that a member of the Governing Council who is prevented from voting for a prolonged period may appoint an alternate as a member of the Governing Council.

Subject to Articles 10.3 and 11.3, each member of the Governing Council shall have one vote. Save as otherwise provided for in this Statute, the Governing Council shall act by a simple majority. In the event of a tie, the President shall have the casting vote.

In order for the Governing Council to vote, there shall be a quorum of two-thirds of the members. If the quorum is not met, the President may convene an extraordinary meeting at which decisions may be taken without regard to the quorum.

10.3. For any decisions to be taken under Articles 28, 29, 30, 32, 33 and 51, the votes in the Governing Council shall be weighted according to the national central banks' shares in the subscribed capital of the ECB. The weights of the votes of the members of the Executive Board shall be zero. A decision requiring a qualified majority shall be adopted if the votes cast in favour represent at least two-thirds of the subscribed capital of the ECB and represent at least half of the shareholders. If a Governor is unable to be present, he may nominate an alternate to cast his weighted vote.

10.4. The proceedings of the meetings shall be confidential. The Governing Council may decide to make the outcome of its deliberations public.

10.5. The Governing Council shall meet at least 10 times a year.

Article 11

The Executive Board

11.1. In accordance with Article 109a(2)(a) of this Treaty, the Executive Board shall comprise the President, the Vice-President and four other members.

The members shall perform their duties on a full-time basis. No member shall engage in any occupation, whether gainful or not, unless exemption is exceptionally granted by the Governing Council.

11.2. In accordance with Article 109a(2)(b) of this Treaty, the President, the Vice-President and the other Members of the Executive Board shall be appointed from among persons of recognized standing and professional experience in monetary or banking matters by common accord of the governments of the Member States at the level of the Heads of State or Government, on a recommendation from the Council after it has consulted the European Parliament and the Governing Council.

Their term of office shall be eight years and shall not be renewable.

Only nationals of Member States may be members of the Executive Board.

11.3. The terms and conditions of employment of the members of the Executive Board, in particular their salaries, pensions and other social security benefits shall be the subject of contracts with the ECB and shall be fixed by the Governing Council on a proposal from a Committee comprising three members appointed by the Governing Council and three members appointed by the Council. The members of the Executive Board shall not have the right to vote on matters referred to in this paragraph.

11.4. If a member of the Executive Board no longer fulfils the conditions required for the performance of his duties or if he has been guilty of serious misconduct, the Court of Justice may, on application by the Governing Council or the Executive Board, compulsorily retire him.

11.5. Each member of the Executive Board present in person shall have the right to vote and shall have, for that purpose, one vote. Save as otherwise provided, the Executive Board shall act by a simple majority of the votes cast. In the event of a tie, the President shall have the casting vote. The voting arrangements shall be specified in the Rules of Procedure referred to in Article 12.3.

11.6. The Executive Board shall be responsible for the current business of the ECB.

11.7. Any vacancy on the Executive Board shall be filled by the appointment of a new member in accordance with Article 11.2.

Article 12

Responsibilities of the decision-making bodies

12.1. The Governing Council shall adopt the guidelines and make the decisions necessary to ensure the performance of the tasks entrusted to the ESCB under this Treaty and this Statute. The Governing Council shall formulate the monetary policy of the Community including, as appropriate, decisions relating to intermediate monetary objectives, key interest rates and the supply of reserves in the ESCB, and shall establish the necessary guidelines for their implementation.

The Executive Board shall implement monetary policy in accordance with the guidelines and decisions laid down by the Governing Council. In doing so the Executive Board shall give the necessary instructions to national central banks. In addition the Executive Board may have certain powers delegated to it where the Governing Council so decides.

To the extent deemed possible and appropriate and without prejudice to the provisions of this Article, the ECB shall have recourse to the national central banks to carry out operations which form part of the tasks of the ESCB.

12.2. The Executive Board shall have responsibility for the preparation of meetings of the Governing Council.

12.3. The Governing Council shall adopt Rules of Procedure which determine the internal organization of the ECB and its decision-making bodies.

12.4. The Governing Council shall exercise the advisory functions referred to in Article 4.

12.5. The Governing Council shall take the decisions referred to in Article 6.

Article 13

The President

13.1. The President or, in his absence, the Vice-President shall chair the Governing Council and the Executive Board of the ECB.

13.2. Without prejudice to Article 39, the President or his nominee shall represent the ECB externally.

Article 14

National central banks

14.1. In accordance with Article 108 of this Treaty, each Member State shall ensure, at the latest at the date of the establishment of the ESCB, that its national legislation, including the statutes of its national central bank, is compatible with this Treaty and this Statute.

14.2. The statutes of the national central banks shall, in particular, provide that the term of office of a Governor of a national central bank shall be no less than five years.

A Governor may be relieved from office only if he no longer fulfils the conditions required for the performance of his duties or if he has been guilty of serious misconduct. A decision to this effect may be referred to the Court of Justice by the Governor concerned or the Governing Council on grounds of infringement of this Treaty or of any rule of law relating to its application. Such proceedings shall be instituted within two months of the publication of the decision or of its notification to the plaintiff or, in the absence thereof, of the day on which it came to the knowledge of the latter, as the case may be.

14.3. The national central banks are an integral part of the ESCB and shall act in accordance with the guidelines and instructions of the ECB. The Governing Council shall take the necessary steps to ensure compliance with the guidelines and instructions of the ECB, and shall require that any necessary information be given to it.

14.4. National central banks may perform functions other than those specified in this Statute unless the Governing Council finds, by a majority of two thirds of the votes cast, that these interfere with the objectives and tasks of the ESCB. Such functions shall be performed on the responsibility and liability of national central banks and shall not be regarded as being part of the functions of the ESCB.

Article 15

Reporting commitments

15.1. The ECB shall draw up and publish reports on the activities of the ESCB at least quarterly.

15.2. A consolidated financial statement of the ESCB shall be published each week.

15.3. In accordance with Article 109b(3) of this Treaty, the ECB shall address an annual report on the activities of the ESCB and on the monetary policy of both the previous and the current year to the European Parliament, the Council and the Commission, and also to the European Council.

15.4. The reports and statements referred to in this Article shall be made available to interested parties free of charge.

Article 16

Banknotes

In accordance with Article 105a(1) of this Treaty, the Governing Council shall have the exclusive right to authorize the issue of banknotes within the Community. The ECB and the national central banks may issue such notes. The banknotes issued by the ECB and the national central banks shall be the only such notes to have the status of legal tender within the Community.

The ECB shall respect as far as possible existing practices regarding the issue and design of banknotes.

CHAPTER IV

MONETARY FUNCTIONS AND OPERATIONS OF THE ESCB

Article 17

Accounts with the ECB and the national central banks

In order to conduct their operations, the ECB and the national central banks may open accounts for credit institutions, public entities and other market participants and accept assets, including book-entry securities, as collateral.

Article 18

Open market and credit operations

18.1. In order to achieve the objectives of the ESCB and to carry out its tasks, the ECB and the national central banks may:

— operate in the financial markets by buying and selling outright (spot and forward) or under repurchase agreement and by lending or borrowing claims and marketable instruments, whether in Community or in non-Community currencies, as well as precious metals;

— conduct credit operations with credit institutions and other market participants, with lending being based on adequate collateral.

18.2. The ECB shall establish general principles for open market and credit operations carried out by itself or the national central banks, including for the announcement of conditions under which they stand ready to enter into such transactions.

Article 19

Minimum reserves

19.1. Subject to Article 2, the ECB may require credit institutions established in Member States to hold minimum reserves on accounts with the ECB and national central banks in pursuance of monetary policy objectives. Regulations concerning the calculation and determination of the required minimum reserves may be established by the Governing Council. In cases of non-compliance the ECB shall be entitled to levy penalty interest and to impose other sanctions with comparable effect.

19.2. For the application of this Article, the Council shall, in accordance with the procedure laid down in Article 42, define the basis for minimum reserves and the maximum permissible ratios between those reserves and their basis, as well as the appropriate sanctions in cases of non-compliance.

Article 20

Other instruments of monetary control

The Governing Council may, by a majority of two thirds of the votes cast, decide upon the use of such other operational methods of monetary control as it sees fit, respecting Article 2.

The Council shall, in accordance with the procedure laid down in Article 42, define the scope of such methods if they impose obligations on third parties.

Article 21

Operations with public entities

21.1. In accordance with Article 104 of this Treaty, overdrafts or any other type of credit facility with the ECB or with the national central banks in favour of Community institutions or bodies, central governments, regional, local or other public authorities, other bodies governed by public law, or public undertakings of Member States shall be prohibited, as shall the purchase directly from them by the ECB or national central banks of debt instruments.

21.2. The ECB and national central banks may act as fiscal agents for the entities referred to in Article 21.1.

21.3. The provisions of this Article shall not apply to publicly-owned credit institutions which, in the context of the supply of reserves by central banks, shall be given the same treatment by national central banks and the ECB as private credit institutions.

Article 22

Clearing and payment systems

The ECB and national central banks may provide facilities, and the ECB may make regulations, to ensure efficient and sound clearing and payment systems within the Community and with other countries.

Article 23

External operations

The ECB and national central banks may:

— establish relations with central banks and financial institutions in other countries and, where appropriate, with international organizations;

— acquire and sell spot and forward all types of foreign exchange assets and precious metals; the term 'foreign exchange asset' shall include securities and all other assets in the currency of any country or units of account and in whatever form held;

— hold and manage the assets referred to in this Article;

— conduct all types of banking transactions in relations with third countries and international organizations, including borrowing and lending operations.

Article 24

Other operations

In addition to operations arising from their tasks, the ECB and national central banks may enter into operations for their administrative purposes or for their staff.

CHAPTER V

PRUDENTIAL SUPERVISION

Article 25

Prudential supervision

25.1. The ECB may offer advice to and be consulted by the Council, the Commission and the competent authorities of the Member States on the scope and implementation of Community legislation relating to the prudential supervision of credit institutions and to the stability of the financial system.

25.2. In accordance with any decision of the Council under Article 105(6) of this Treaty, the ECB may perform specific tasks concerning policies relating to the prudential supervision of credit institutions and other financial institutions with the exception of insurance undertakings.

CHAPTER VI

FINANCIAL PROVISIONS OF THE ESCB

Article 26

Financial accounts

26.1. The financial year of the ECB and national central banks shall begin on the first day of January and end on the last day of December.

26.2. The annual accounts of the ECB shall be drawn up by the Executive Board, in accordance with the principles established by the Governing Council. The accounts shall be approved by the Governing Council and shall thereafter be published.

26.3. For analytical and operational purposes, the Executive Board shall draw up a consolidated balance sheet of the ESCB, comprising those assets and liabilities of the national central banks that fall within the ESCB.

26.4. For the application of this Article, the Governing Council shall establish the necessary rules for standardizing the accounting and reporting of operations undertaken by the national central banks.

Article 27

Auditing

27.1. The accounts of the ECB and national central banks shall be audited by independent external auditors recommended by the Governing Council and approved by the Council. The auditors shall have full power to examine all books and accounts of the ECB and national central banks and obtain full information about their transactions.

27.2. The provisions of Article 188c of this Treaty shall only apply to an examination of the operational efficiency of the management of the ECB.

Article 28

Capital of the ECB

28.1. The capital of the ECB, which shall become operational upon its establishment, shall be ecu 5 000 million. The capital may be increased by such amounts as may be decided by the Governing Council acting by the qualified majority provided for in Article 10.3, within the limits and under the conditions set by the Council under the procedure laid down in Article 42.

28.2. The national central banks shall be the sole subscribers to and holders of the capital of the ECB. The subscription of capital shall be according to the key established in accordance with Article 29.

28.3. The Governing Council, acting by the qualified majority provided for in Article 10.3, shall determine the extent to which and the form in which the capital shall be paid up.

28.4. Subject to Article 28.5, the shares of the national central banks in the subscribed capital of the ECB may not be transferred, pledged or attached.

28.5. If the key referred to in Article 29 is adjusted, the national central banks shall transfer among themselves capital shares to the extent necessary to ensure that the distribution of capital shares corresponds to the adjusted key. The Governing Council shall determine the terms and conditions of such transfers.

Article 29

Key for capital subscription

29.1. When in accordance with the procedure referred to in Article 109*l*(1) of this Treaty the ESCB and the ECB have been established, the key for subscription of the ECB's capital shall be established. Each national central bank shall be assigned a weighting in this key which shall be equal to the sum of:

— 50 % of the share of its respective Member State in the population of the Community in the penultimate year preceding the establishment of the ESCB;

— 50 % of the share of its respective Member State in the gross domestic product at market prices of the Community as recorded in the last five years preceding the penultimate year before the establishment of the ESCB;

The percentages shall be rounded up to the nearest multiple of 0.05 percentage points.

29.2. The statistical data to be used for the application of this Article shall be provided by the Commission in accordance with the rules adopted by the Council under the procedure provided for in Article 42.

29.3. The weightings assigned to the national central banks shall be adjusted every five years after the establishment of the ESCB by analogy with the provisions laid down in Article 29.1. The adjusted key shall apply with effect from the first day of the following year.

29.4. The Governing Council shall take all other measures necessary for the application of this Article.

Article 30

Transfer of foreign reserve assets to the ECB

30.1. Without prejudice to Article 28, the ECB shall be provided by the national central banks with foreign reserve assets, other than Member States' currencies, ecus, IMF reserve positions and SDRs, up to an amount equivalent to ECU 50 000 million. The Governing Council shall decide upon the proportion to be called up by the ECB following its establishment and the amounts called up at later dates. The ECB shall have the full right to hold and manage the foreign reserves that are transferred to it and to use them for the purposes set out in this Statute.

30.2. The contributions of each national central bank shall be fixed in proportion to its share in the subscribed capital of the ECB.

30.3. Each national central bank shall be credited by the ECB with a claim equivalent to its contribution. The Governing Council shall determine the denomination and remuneration of such claims.

30.4. Further calls of foreign reserve assets beyond the limit set in Article 30.1 may be effected by the ECB, in accordance with Article 30.2, within the limits and under the conditions set by the Council in accordance with the procedure laid down in Article 42.

30.5. The ECB may hold and manage IMF reserve positions and SDRs and provide for the pooling of such assets.

30.6. The Governing Council shall take all other measures necessary for the application of this Article.

Article 31

Foreign reserve assets held by national central banks

31.1. The national central banks shall be allowed to perform transactions in fulfilment of their obligations towards international organizations in accordance with Article 23.

31.2. All other operations in foreign reserve assets remaining with the national central banks after the transfers referred to in Article 30, and Member States' transactions with their foreign exchange working balances shall, above a certain limit to be established within the framework of Article 31.3, be subject to approval by the ECB in order to ensure consistency with the exchange rate and monetary policies of the Community.

31.3. The Governing Council shall issue guidelines with a view to facilitating such operations.

Article 32

Allocation of monetary income of national central banks

32.1. The income accruing to the national central banks in the performance of the ESCB's monetary policy function (hereinafter referred to as 'monetary income') shall be allocated at the end of each financial year in accordance with the provisions of this Article.

32.2. Subject to Article 32.3, the amount of each national central bank's monetary income shall be equal to its annual income derived from its assets held against notes in circulation and deposit liabilities to credit institutions. These assets shall be earmarked by national central banks in accordance with guidelines to be established by the Governing Council.

32.3. If, after the start of the third stage, the balance sheet structures of the national central banks do not, in the judgment of the Governing Council, permit the application of Article 32.2, the Governing Council, acting by a qualified majority, may decide that, by way of derogation from Article 32.2, monetary income shall be measured according to an alternative method for a period of not more than five years.

32.4. The amount of each national central bank's monetary income shall be reduced by an amount equivalent to any interest paid by that central bank on its deposit liabilities to credit institutions in accordance with Article 19.

The Governing Council may decide that national central banks shall be indemnified against costs incurred in connection with the issue of banknotes or in exceptional circumstances for specific losses arising from monetary policy operations undertaken for the ESCB. Indemnification shall be in a form deemed appropriate in the judgment of the Governing Council; these amounts may be offset against the national central banks' monetary income.

32.5. The sum of the national central banks' monetary income shall be allocated to the national central banks in proportion to their paid-up shares in the capital of the ECB, subject to any decision taken by the Governing Council pursuant to Article 33.2.

32.6. The clearing and settlement of the balances arising from the allocation of monetary income shall be carried out by the ECB in accordance with guidelines established by the Governing Council.

32.7. The Governing Council shall take all other measures necessary for the application of this Article.

Article 33

Allocation of net profits and losses of the ECB

33.1. The net profit of the ECB shall be transferred in the following order:

(a) an amount to be determined by the Governing Council, which may not exceed 20% of the net profit, shall be transferred to the general reserve fund subject to a limit equal to 100% of the capital;

(b) the remaining net profit shall be distributed to the shareholders of the ECB in proportion to their paid-up shares.

33.2. In the event of a loss incurred by the ECB, the shortfall may be offset against the general reserve fund of the ECB and, if necessary, following a decision by the Governing Council, against the monetary income of the relevant financial year in proportion and up to the amounts allocated to the national central banks in accordance with Article 32.5.

CHAPTER VII

GENERAL PROVISIONS

Article 34

Legal acts

34.1. In accordance with Article 108a of this Treaty, the ECB shall:

— make regulations to the extent necessary to implement the tasks defined in Article 3.1, first indent, Articles 19.1, 22 or 25.2 and in cases which shall be laid down in the acts of the Council referred to in Article 42;

— take decisions necessary for carrying out the tasks entrusted to the ESCB under this Treaty and this Statute;

— make recommendations and deliver opinions.

34.2. A regulation shall have general application. It shall be binding in its entirety and directly applicable in all Member States.

Recommendations and opinions shall have no binding force.

A decision shall be binding in its entirety upon those to whom it is addressed.

Articles 190 to 192 of this Treaty shall apply to regulations and decisions adopted by the ECB.

The ECB may decide to publish its decisions, recommendations and opinions.

34.3. Within the limits and under the conditions adopted by the Council under the procedure laid down in Article 42, the ECB shall be entitled to impose fines or periodic penalty payments on undertakings for failure to comply with obligations under its regulations and decisions.

Article 35

Judicial control and related matters

35.1. The acts or omissions of the ECB shall be open to review or interpretation by the Court of Justice in the cases and under the conditions laid down in this Treaty. The ECB may institute proceedings in the cases and under the conditions laid down in this Treaty.

35.2. Disputes between the ECB, on the one hand, and its creditors, debtors or any other person, on the other, shall be decided by the competent national courts, save where jurisdiction has been conferred upon the Court of Justice.

35.3. The ECB shall be subject to the liability regime provided for in Article 215 of this Treaty. The national central banks shall be liable according to their respective national laws.

35.4. The Court of Justice shall have jurisdiction to give judgment pursuant to any arbitration clause contained in a contract concluded by or on behalf of the ECB, whether that contract be governed by public or private law.

35.5. A decision of the ECB to bring an action before the Court of Justice shall be taken by the Governing Council.

35.6. The Court of Justice shall have jurisdiction in disputes concerning the fulfilment by a national central bank of obligations under this Statute. If the ECB considers that a national central bank has failed to fulfil an obligation under this Statute, it shall deliver a reasoned opinion on the matter after giving the national central bank concerned the opportunity to submit its observations. If the national central bank concerned does not comply with the opinion within the period laid down by the ECB, the latter may bring the matter before the Court of Justice.

Article 36

Staff

36.1. The Governing Council, on a proposal from the Executive Board, shall lay down the conditions of employment of the staff of the ECB.

36.2. The Court of Justice shall have jurisdiction in any dispute between the ECB and its servants within the limits and under the conditions laid down in the conditions of employment.

Article 37

Seat

Before the end of 1992, the decision as to where the seat of the ECB will be established shall be taken by common accord of the governments of the Member States at the level of Heads of State or Government.

Article 38

Professional secrecy

38.1. Members of the governing bodies and the staff of the ECB and the national central banks shall be required, even after their duties have ceased, not to disclose information of the kind covered by the obligation of professional secrecy.

38.2. Persons having access to data covered by Community legislation imposing an obligation of secrecy shall be subject to such legislation.

Article 39

Signatories

The ECB shall be legally committed to third parties by the President or by two members of the Executive Board or by the signatures of two members of the staff of the ECB who have been duly authorized by the President to sign on behalf of the ECB.

Article 40

Privileges and immunities

The ECB shall enjoy in the territories of the Member States such privileges and immunities as are necessary for the performance of its tasks, under the conditions laid down in the Protocol on the Privileges and Immunities of the European Communities annexed to the Treaty establishing a Single Council and a Single Commission of the European Communities.

CHAPTER VIII

AMENDMENT OF THE STATUTE AND COMPLEMENTARY LEGISLATION

Article 41

Simplified amendment procedure

41.1. In accordance with Article 106(5) of this Treaty, Articles 5.1, 5.2, 5.3, 17, 18, 19.1, 22, 23, 24, 26, 32.2, 32.3, 32.4, 32.6, 33.1(a) and 36 of this Statute may be amended by the Council, acting either by a qualified majority on a recommendation from the ECB and after consulting the Commission, or unanimously on a proposal from the Commission and after consulting the ECB. In either case the assent of the European Parliament shall be required.

41.2. A recommendation made by the ECB under this Article shall require a unanimous decision by the Governing Council.

Article 42

Complementary legislation

In accordance with Article 106(6) of this Treaty, immediately after the decision on the date for the beginning of the third stage, the Council, acting by a qualified majority either on a proposal from the Commission and after consulting the European Parliament and the ECB or on a recommendation from the ECB and after consulting the European Parliament and the Commission, shall adopt the provisions referred to in Articles 4, 5.4, 19.2, 20, 28.1, 29.2, 30.4 and 34.3 of this Statute.

CHAPTER IX

TRANSITIONAL AND OTHER PROVISIONS FOR THE ESCB

Article 43

General provisions

43.1. A derogation as referred to in Article 109k(1) of this Treaty shall entail that the following Articles of this Statute shall not confer any rights or impose any obligations on the Member State concerned: 3, 6, 9.2, 12.1, 14.3, 16, 18, 19, 20, 22, 23, 26.2, 27, 30, 31, 32, 33, 34, 50 and 52.

43.2. The central banks of Member States with a derogation as specified in Article 109k(1) of this Treaty shall retain their powers in the field of monetary policy according to national law.

43.3. In accordance with Article 109k(4) of this Treaty, 'Member States' shall be read as 'Member States without a derogation' in the following Articles of this Statute: 3, 11.2, 19, 34.2 and 50.

43.4. 'National central banks' shall be read as 'central banks of Member States without a derogation' in the following Articles of this Statute: 9.2, 10.1, 10.3, 12.1, 16, 17, 18, 22, 23, 27, 30, 31, 32, 33.2 and 52.

43.5. 'Shareholders' shall be read as 'central banks of Member States without a derogation' in Articles 10.3 and 33.1.

43.6. 'Subscribed capital of the ECB' shall be read as 'capital of the ECB subscribed by the central banks of Member States without a derogation' in Articles 10.3 and 30.2.

Article 44

Transitional tasks of the ECB

The ECB shall take over those tasks of the EMI which, because of the derogations of one or more Member States, still have to be performed in the third stage.

The ECB shall give advice in the preparations for the abrogation of the derogations specified in Article 109k of this Treaty.

Article 45

The General Council of the ECB

45.1. Without prejudice to Article 106(3) of this Treaty, the General Council shall be constituted as a third decision-making body of the ECB.

45.2. The General Council shall comprise the President and Vice-President of the ECB and the Governors of the national central banks. The other members of the Executive Board may participate, without having the right to vote, in meetings of the General Council.

45.3. The responsibilities of the General Council are listed in full in Article 47 of this Statute.

Article 46

Rules of procedure of the General Council

46.1. The President or, in his absence, the Vice-President of the ECB shall chair the General Council of the ECB.

46.2. The President of the Council and a member of the Commission may participate, without having the right to vote, in meetings of the General Council.

46.3. The President shall prepare the meetings of the General Council.

46.4. By way of derogation from Article 12.3, the General Council shall adopt its Rules of Procedure.

46.5. The Secretariat of the General Council shall be provided by the ECB.

Article 47

Responsibilities of the General Council

47.1. The General Council shall:

— perform the tasks referred to in Article 44;

— contribute to the advisory functions referred to in Articles 4 and 25.1.

47.2. The General Council shall contribute to:

— the collection of statistical information as referred to in Article 5;

— the reporting activities of the ECB as referred to in Article 15;

— the establishment of the necessary rules for the application of Article 26 as referred to in Article 26.4;

— the taking of all other measures necessary for the application of Article 29 as referred to in Article 29.4;

— the laying down of the conditions of employment of the staff of the ECB as referred to in Article 36.

47.3. The General Council shall contribute to the necessary preparations for irrevocably fixing the exchange rates of the currencies of Member States with a derogation against the currencies, or the single currency, of the Member States without a derogation, as referred to in Article 109l(5) of this Treaty.

47.4. The General Council shall be informed by the President of the ECB of decisions of the Governing Council.

Article 48

Transitional provisions for the capital of the ECB

In accordance with Article 29.1 each national central bank shall be assigned a weighting in the key for subscription of the ECB's capital. By way of derogation from Article 28.3, central banks of Member States with a derogation shall not pay up their subscribed capital unless the General Council, acting by a majority representing at least two-thirds of the subscribed capital of the ECB and at least half of the shareholders, decides that a minimal percentage has to be paid up as a contribution to the operational costs of the ECB.

Article 49

Deferred payment of capital, reserves and provisions of the ECB

49.1. The central bank of a Member State whose derogation has been abrogated shall pay up its subscribed share of the capital of the ECB to the same extent as the central banks of other Member States without a derogation, and shall transfer to the ECB foreign reserve assets in accordance with Article 30.1. The sum to be transferred shall be determined by multiplying the ecu value at current exchange rates of the foreign reserve assets which have already been transferred to the ECB in accordance with Article 30.1, by the ratio between the number of shares subscribed by the national central bank concerned and the number of shares already paid up by the other national central banks.

49.2. In addition to the payment to be made in accordance with Article 49.1, the central bank concerned shall contribute to the reserves of the ECB, to those provisions equivalent to reserves, and to the amount still to be appropriated to the reserves and provisions corresponding to the balance of the profit and loss account as at 31 December of the year prior to the abrogation of the derogation. The sum to be contributed shall be determined by multiplying the amount of the reserves, as defined above and as stated in the approved balance sheet of the ECB, by the ratio between the number of shares subscribed by the central bank concerned and the number of shares already paid up by the other central banks.

Article 50

Initial appointment of the members of the Executive Board

When the Executive Board of the ECB is being established, the President, the Vice-President and the other members of the Executive Board shall be appointed by common accord of the governments of the Member States at the level of Heads of State or Government, on a recommendation from the Council and after consulting the European Parliament and the Council of the EMI. The President of the Executive Board shall be appointed for eight years. By way of derogation from Article 11.2, the Vice-President shall be appointed for four years and the other members of the Executive Board for terms of office of between five and eight years. No term of office shall be renewable. The number of members of the Executive Board may be smaller than provided for in Article 11.1, but in no circumstance shall it be less than four.

Article 51

Derogation from Article 32

51.1. If, after the start of the third stage, the Governing Council decides that the application of Article 32 results in significant changes in national central banks' relative income positions, the amount of income to be allocated pursuant to Article 32 shall be reduced by a uniform percentage which shall not exceed 60% in the first financial year after the start of the third stage and which shall decrease by at least 12 percentage points in each subsequent financial year.

51.2. Article 51.1 shall be applicable for not more than five financial years after the start of the third stage.

Article 52

Exchange of banknotes in Community currencies

Following the irrevocable fixing of exchange rates, the Governing Council shall take the necessary measures to ensure that banknotes denominated in currencies with irrevocably fixed exchange rates are exchanged by the national central banks at their respective par values.

Article 53

Applicability of the transitional provisions

If and as long as there are Member States with a derogation Articles 43 to 48 shall be applicable.

PROTOCOL

ON THE STATUTE OF THE EUROPEAN MONETARY INSTITUTE

THE HIGH CONTRACTING PARTIES,

DESIRING to lay down the Statute of the European Monetary Institute,

HAVE AGREED upon the following provisions, which shall be annexed to the Treaty establishing the European Community:

Article 1

Constitution and name

1.1. The European Monetary Institute (EMI) shall be established in accordance with Article 109f of this Treaty; it shall perform its functions and carry out its activities in accordance with the provisions of this Treaty and of this Statute.

1.2. The members of the EMI shall be the central banks of the Member States ('national central banks'). For the purposes of this Statute, the Institut monétaire luxembourgeois shall be regarded as the central bank of Luxembourg.

1.3. Pursuant to Article 109f of this Treaty, both the Committee of Governors and the European Monetary Cooperation Fund (EMCF) shall be dissolved. All assets and liabilities of the EMCF shall pass automatically to the EMI.

Article 2

Objectives

The EMI shall contribute to the realization of the conditions necessary for the transition to the third stage of economic and monetary union, in particular by:

— strengthening the coordination of monetary policies with a view to ensuring price stability;

— making the preparations required for the establishment of the European System of Central Banks (ESCB), and for the conduct of a single monetary policy and the creation of a single currency in the third stage;

— overseeing the development of the ecu.

Article 3

General principles

3.1. The EMI shall carry out the tasks and functions conferred upon it by this Treaty and this Statute without prejudice to the responsibility of the competent authorities for the conduct of the monetary policy within the respective Member States.

3.2. The EMI shall act in accordance with the objectives and principles stated in Article 2 of the Statute of the ESCB.

Article 4

Primary tasks

4.1. In accordance with Article 109f(2) of this Treaty, the EMI shall:

— strengthen cooperation between the national central banks;

— strengthen the coordination of the monetary policies of the Member States with the aim of ensuring price stability;

— monitor the functioning of the European Monetary System (EMS);

— hold consultations concerning issues falling within the competence of the national central banks and affecting the stability of financial institutions and markets;

— take over the tasks of the EMCF; in particular it shall perform the functions referred to in Articles 6.1, 6.2 and 6.3;

— facilitate the use of the ecu and oversee its development, including the smooth functioning of the ecu clearing system.

The EMI shall also:

— hold regular consultations concerning the course of monetary policies and the use of monetary policy instruments;

— normally be consulted by the national monetary authorities before they take decisions on the course of monetary policy in the context of the common framework for *ex ante* coordination.

4.2. At the latest by 31 December 1996, the EMI shall specify the regulatory, organizational and logistical framework necessary for the ESCB to perform its tasks in the third stage, in accordance with the principle of an open market economy with free competition. This framework shall be submitted by the Council of the EMI for decision to the ECB at the date of its establishment.

In accordance with Article 109f(3) of this Treaty, the EMI shall in particular:

— prepare the instruments and the procedures necessary for carrying out a single monetary policy in the third stage;

— promote the harmonization, where necessary, of the rules and practices governing the collection, compilation and distribution of statistics in the areas within its field of competence;

— prepare the rules for operations to be undertaken by the national central banks in the framework of the ESCB;

— promote the efficiency of cross-border payments;

— supervise the technical preparation of ecu banknotes.

Article 5

Advisory functions

5.1. In accordance with Article 109f(4) of this Treaty, the Council of the EMI may formulate opinions or recommendations on the overall orientation of monetary policy and exchange-rate policy as well as on related measures introduced in each Member State. The EMI may submit opinions or recommendations to governments and to the Council on policies which might affect the internal or external monetary situation in the Community and, in particular, the functioning of the EMS.

5.2. The Council of the EMI may also make recommendations to the monetary authorities of the Member States concerning the conduct of their monetary policy.

5.3. In accordance with Article 109f(6) of this Treaty, the EMI shall be consulted by the Council regarding any proposed Community act within its field of competence.

Within the limits and under the conditions set out by the Council acting by a qualified majority on a proposal from the Commission and after consulting the European Parliament and the EMI, the EMI shall be consulted by the authorities of the Member States on any draft legislative provision within its field of competence, in particular with regard to Article 4.2.

5.4. In accordance with Article 109f(5) of this Treaty, the EMI may decide to publish its opinions and its recommendations.

Article 6

Operational and technical functions

6.1. The EMI shall:

— provide for the multilateralization of positions resulting from interventions by the national central banks in Community currencies and the multilateralization of intra-Community settlements;

— administer the very short-term financing mechanism provided for by the Agreement of 13 March 1979 between the central banks of the Member States of the European Economic Community laying down the operating procedures for the European Monetary System (hereinafter referred to as 'EMS Agreement') and the short-term monetary support mechanism provided for in the Agreement between the central banks of the Member States of the European Economic Community of 9 February 1970, as amended;

— perform the functions referred to in Article 11 of Council Regulation (EEC) No 1969/88 of 24 June 1988 establishing a single facility providing medium-term financial assistance for Member States' balances of payments.

6.2. The EMI may receive monetary reserves from the national central banks and issue ecus against such assets for the purpose of implementing the EMS Agreement. These ecus may be used by the EMI and the national central banks as a means of settlement and for transactions between them and the EMI. The EMI shall take the necessary administrative measures for the implementation of this paragraph.

6.3. The EMI may grant to the monetary authorities of third countries and to international monetary institutions the status of 'other holders' of ecus and fix the terms and conditions under which such ecus may be acquired, held or used by other holders.

6.4. The EMI shall be entitled to hold and manage foreign exchange reserves as an agent for and at the request of national central banks. Profits and losses regarding these reserves shall be for the account of the national central bank depositing the reserves. The EMI shall perform this function on the basis of bilateral contracts in accordance with rules laid down in a decision of the EMI. These rules shall ensure that transactions with these reserves shall not interfere with the monetary policy and exchange-rate policy of the competent monetary authority of any Member State and shall be consistent with the objectives of the EMI and the proper functioning of the exchange-rate mechanism of the EMS.

Article 7

Other tasks

7.1. Once a year the EMI shall address a report to the Council on the state of the preparations for the third stage. These reports shall include an assessment of the progress towards convergence in the Community, and cover in particular the adaptation of monetary policy instruments and the preparation of the procedures necessary for carrying out a single monetary policy in the third stage, as well as the statutory requirements to be fulfilled for national central banks to become an integral part of the ESCB.

7.2. In accordance with the Council decisions referred to in Article 109f(7) of this Treaty, the EMI may perform other tasks for the preparation of the third stage.

Article 8

Independence

The members of the Council of the EMI who are the representatives of their institutions shall, with respect to their activities, act according to their own responsibilities. In exercising the powers and performing the tasks and duties conferred upon them by this Treaty and this Statute, the Council of the EMI may not seek or take any instructions from Community institutions or bodies or governments of Member States. The Community institutions and bodies as well as the governments of the Member States undertake to respect this principle and not to seek to influence the Council of the EMI in the performance of its tasks.

Article 9

Administration

9.1. In accordance with Article 109f(1) of this Treaty, the EMI shall be directed and managed by the Council of the EMI.

9.2. The Council of the EMI shall consist of a President and the Governors of the national central banks, one of whom shall be Vice-President. If a Governor is prevented from attending a meeting, he may nominate another representative of his institution.

9.3. The President shall be appointed by common accord of the governments of the Member States at the level of Heads of State or Government, on a recommendation from, as the case may be, the Committee of Governors or the Council of the EMI, and after consulting the European Parliament and the Council. The President shall be selected from among persons of recognized standing and professional experience in monetary or banking matters. Only nationals of Member States may be President of the EMI. The Council of the EMI shall appoint the Vice-President. The President and Vice-President shall be appointed for a period of three years.

9.4. The President shall perform his duties on a full-time basis. He shall not engage in any occupation, whether gainful or not, unless exemption is exceptionally granted by the Council of the EMI.

9.5. The President shall:

— prepare and chair the meetings of the Council of the EMI;

— without prejudice to Article 22, present the views of the EMI externally;

— be responsible for the day-to-day management of the EMI.

In the absence of the President, his duties shall be performed by the Vice-President.

9.6. The terms and conditions of employment of the President, in particular his salary, pension and other social security benefits, shall be the subject of a contract with the EMI and shall be fixed by the Council of the EMI on a proposal from a Committee comprising three members appointed by the Committee of Governors or the Council of the EMI, as the case may be, and three members appointed by the Council. The President shall not have the right to vote on matters referred to in this paragraph.

9.7. If the President no longer fulfils the conditions required for the performance of his duties or if he has been guilty of serious misconduct, the Court of Justice may, on application by the Council of the EMI, compulsorily retire him.

9.8. The Rules of Procedure of the EMI shall be adopted by the Council of the EMI.

Article 10

Meetings of the Council of the EMI and voting procedures

10.1. The Council of the EMI shall meet at least 10 times a year. The proceedings of Council meetings shall be confidential. The Council of the EMI may, acting unanimously, decide to make the outcome of its deliberations public.

10.2. Each member of the Council of the EMI or his nominee shall have one vote.

10.3. Save as otherwise provided for in this Statute, the Council of the EMI shall act by a simple majority of its members.

10.4. Decisions to be taken in the context of Articles 4.2, 5.4, 6.2 and 6.3 shall require unanimity of the members of the Council of the EMI.

The adoption of opinions and recommendations under Articles 5.1 and 5.2, the adoption of decisions under Articles 6.4, 16 and 23.6 and the adoption of guidelines under Article 15.3 shall require a qualified majority of two thirds of the members of the Council of the EMI.

Article 11

Interinstitutional cooperation and reporting requirements

11.1. The President of the Council and a member of the Commission may participate, without having the right to vote, in meetings of the Council of the EMI.

11.2. The President of the EMI shall be invited to participate in Council meetings when the Council is discussing matters relating to the objectives and tasks of the EMI.

11.3. At a date to be established in the Rules of Procedure, the EMI shall prepare an annual report on its activities and on monetary and financial conditions in the Community. The annual report, together with the annual accounts of the EMI, shall be addressed to the European Parliament, the Council and the Commission and also to the European Council.

The President of the EMI may, at the request of the European Parliament or on his own initiative, be heard by the competent Committees of the European Parliament.

11.4. Reports published by the EMI shall be made available to interested parties free of charge.

Article 12

Currency denomination

The operations of the EMI shall be expressed in ecus.

Article 13

Seat

Before the end of 1992, the decision as to where the seat of the EMI will be established shall be taken by common accord of the governments of the Member States at the level of Heads of State or Government.

Article 14

Legal capacity

The EMI, which in accordance with Article 109f(1) of this Treaty shall have legal personality, shall enjoy in each of the Member States the most extensive legal capacity accorded to legal persons under their law; it may, in particular, acquire or dispose of movable or immovable property and may be a party to legal proceedings.

Article 15

Legal acts

15.1. In the performance of its tasks, and under the conditions laid down in this Statute, the EMI shall:

— deliver opinions;

— make recommendations;

— adopt guidelines, and take decisions, which shall be addressed to the national central banks.

15.2. Opinions and recommendations of the EMI shall have no binding force.

15.3. The Council of the EMI may adopt guidelines laying down the methods for the implementation of the conditions necessary for the ESCB to perform its functions in the third stage. EMI guidelines shall have no binding force; they shall be submitted for decision to the ECB.

15.4. Without prejudice to Article 3.1, a decision of the EMI shall be binding in its entirety upon those to whom it is addressed. Articles 190 and 191 of this Treaty shall apply to these decisions.

Article 16

Financial resources

16.1. The EMI shall be endowed with its own resources. The size of the resources of the EMI shall be determined by the Council of the EMI with a view to ensuring the income deemed necessary to cover the administrative expenditure incurred in the performance of the tasks and functions of the EMI.

16.2. The resources of the EMI determined in accordance with Article 16.1 shall be provided out of contributions by the national central banks in accordance with the key referred to in Article 29.1 of the Statute of the ESCB and be paid up at the establishment of the EMI. For this purpose, the statistical data to be used for the determination of the key shall be provided by the Commission, in accordance with the rules adopted by the Council, acting by a qualified majority on a proposal from the Commission and after consulting the European Parliament, the Committee of Governors and the Committee referred to in Article 109c of this Treaty.

16.3. The Council of the EMI shall determine the form in which contributions shall be paid up.

Article 17

Annual accounts and auditing

17.1. The financial year of the EMI shall begin on the first day of January and end on the last day of December.

17.2. The Council of the EMI shall adopt an annual budget before the beginning of each financial year.

17.3. The annual accounts shall be drawn up in accordance with the principles established by the Council of the EMI. The annual accounts shall be approved by the Council of the EMI and shall thereafter be published.

17.4. The annual accounts shall be audited by independent external auditors approved by the Council of the EMI. The auditors shall have full power to examine all books and accounts of the EMI and to obtain full information about its transactions.

The provisions of Article 188c of this Treaty shall only apply to an examination of the operational efficiency of the management of the EMI.

17.5. Any surplus of the EMI shall be transferred in the following order:

(a) an amount to be determined by the Council of the EMI shall be transferred to the general reserve fund of the EMI;

(b) any remaining surplus shall be distributed to the national central banks in accordance with the key referred to in Article 16.2.

17.6. In the event of a loss incurred by the EMI, the shortfall shall be offset against the general reserve fund of the EMI. Any remaining shortfall shall be made good by contributions from the national central banks, in accordance with the key as referred to in Article 16.2.

Article 18

Staff

18.1. The Council of the EMI shall lay down the conditions of employment of the staff of the EMI.

18.2. The Court of Justice shall have jurisdiction in any dispute between the EMI and its servants within the limits and under the conditions laid down in the conditions of employment.

Article 19

Judicial control and related matters

19.1. The acts or omissions of the EMI shall be open to review or interpretation by the Court of Justice in the cases and under the conditions laid down in this Treaty. The EMI may institute proceedings in the cases and under the conditions laid down in this Treaty.

19.2. Disputes between the EMI, on the one hand, and its creditors, debtors or any other person, on the other, shall fall within the jurisdiction of the competent national courts, save where jurisdiction has been conferred upon the Court of Justice.

19.3. The EMI shall be subject to the liability regime provided for in Article 215 of this Treaty.

19.4. The Court of Justice shall have jurisdiction to give judgment pursuant to any arbitration clause contained in a contract concluded by or on behalf of the EMI, whether that contract be governed by public or private law.

19.5. A decision of the EMI to bring an action before the Court of Justice shall be taken by the Council of the EMI.

Article 20

Professional secrecy

20.1. Members of the Council of the EMI and the staff of the EMI shall be required, even after their duties have ceased, not to disclose information of the kind covered by the obligation of professional secrecy.

20.2. Persons having access to data covered by Community legislation imposing an obligation of secrecy shall be subject to such legislation.

Article 21

Privileges and immunities

The EMI shall enjoy in the territories of the Member States such privileges and immunities as are necessary for the performance of its tasks, under the conditions laid down in the Protocol on the Privileges and Immunities of the European Communities annexed to the Treaty establishing a Single Council and a Single Commission of the European Communities.

Article 22

Signatories

The EMI shall be legally committed to third parties by the President or the Vice-President or by the signatures of two members of the staff of the EMI who have been duly authorized by the President to sign on behalf of the EMI.

Article 23

Liquidation of the EMI

23.1. In accordance with Article 109*l* of this Treaty, the EMI shall go into liquidation on the establishment of the ECB. All assets and liabilities of the EMI shall then pass automatically to the ECB. The latter shall liquidate the EMI according to the provisions of this Article. The liquidation shall be completed by the beginning of the third stage.

23.2. The mechanism for the creation of ecus against gold and US dollars as provided for by Article 17 of the EMS Agreement shall be unwound by the first day of the third stage in accordance with Article 20 of the said Agreement.

23.3. All claims and liabilities arising from the very short-term financing mechanism and the short-term monetary support mechanism, under the Agreements referred to in Article 6.1, shall be settled by the first day of the third stage.

23.4. All remaining assets of the EMI shall be disposed of and all remaining liabilities of the EMI shall be settled.

23.5. The proceeds of the liquidation described in Article 23.4 shall be distributed to the national central banks in accordance with the key referred to in Article 16.2.

23.6. The Council of the EMI may take the measures necessary for the application of Articles 23.4 and 23.5.

23.7. Upon the establishment of the ECB, the President of the EMI shall relinquish his office.

PROTOCOL

ON THE EXCESSIVE DEFICIT PROCEDURE

THE HIGH CONTRACTING PARTIES,

DESIRING to lay down the details of the excessive deficit procedure referred to in Article 104c of the Treaty establishing the European Community,

HAVE AGREED upon the following provisions, which shall be annexed to the Treaty establishing the European Community:

Article 1

The reference values referred to in Article 104c(2) of this Treaty are:

— 3 % for the ratio of the planned or actual government deficit to gross domestic product at market prices;

— 60 % for the ratio of government debt to gross domestic product at market prices.

Article 2

In Article 104c of this Treaty and in this Protocol:

— government means general government, that is central government, regional or local government and social security funds, to the exclusion of commercial operations, as defined in the European System of Integrated Economic Accounts;

— deficit means net borrowing as defined in the European System of Integrated Economic Accounts;

— investment means gross fixed capital formation as defined in the European System of Integrated Economic Accounts;

— debt means total gross debt at nominal value outstanding at the end of the year and consolidated between and within the sectors of general government as defined in the first indent.

Article 3

In order to ensure the effectiveness of the excessive deficit procedure, the governments of the Member States shall be responsible under this procedure for the deficits of general government as defined in the first indent of Article 2. The Member States shall ensure that national procedures in the budgetary area enable them to meet their obligations in this area deriving from this Treaty. The Member States shall report their planned and actual deficits and the levels of their debt promptly and regularly to the Commission.

Article 4

The statistical data to be used for the application of this Protocol shall be provided by the Commission.

PROTOCOL

ON THE CONVERGENCE CRITERIA REFERRED TO IN ARTICLE 109j OF THE TREATY ESTABLISHING THE EUROPEAN COMMUNITY

THE HIGH CONTRACTING PARTIES,

DESIRING to lay down the details of the convergence criteria which shall guide the Community in taking decisions on the passage to the third stage of economic and monetary union, referred to in Article 109j(1) of this Treaty,

HAVE AGREED upon the following provisions, which shall be annexed to the Treaty establishing the European Community:

Article 1

The criterion on price stability referred to in the first indent of Article 109j(1) of this Treaty shall mean that a Member State has a price performance that is sustainable and an average rate of inflation, observed over a period of one year before the examination, that does not exceed by more than 1½ percentage points that of, at most, the three best performing Member States in terms of price stability. Inflation shall be measured by means of the consumer price index on a comparable basis, taking into account differences in national definitions.

Article 2

The criterion on the government budgetary position referred to in the second indent of Article 109j(1) of this Treaty shall mean that at the time of the examination the Member State is not the subject of a Council decision under Article 104c(6) of this Treaty that an excessive deficit exists.

Article 3

The criterion on participation in the exchange-rate mechanism of the European Monetary System referred to in the third indent of Article 109j(1) of this Treaty shall mean that a Member State has respected the normal fluctuation margins provided for by the exchange-rate mechanism of the European Monetary System without severe tensions for at least the last two years before the examination. In particular, the Member State shall not have devalued its currency's bilateral central rate against any other Member State's currency on its own initiative for the same period.

Article 4

The criterion on the convergence of interest rates referred to in the fourth indent of Article 109j(1) of this Treaty shall mean that, observed over a period of one year before the examination, a Member State has had an average nominal long-term interest rate that does not exceed by more than two percentage points that of, at most, the three best performing Member States in terms of price stability. Interest rates shall be measured on the basis of long-term government bonds or comparable securities, taking into account differences in national definitions.

Article 5

The statistical data to be used for the application of this Protocol shall be provided by the Commission.

Article 6

The Council shall, acting unanimously on a proposal from the Commission and after consulting the European Parliament, the EMI or the ECB as the case may be, and the Committee referred to in Article 109c, adopt appropriate provisions to lay down the details of the convergence criteria referred to in Article 109j of this Treaty, which shall then replace this Protocol.

PROTOCOL

AMENDING THE PROTOCOL
ON THE PRIVILEGES AND IMMUNITIES
OF THE EUROPEAN COMMUNITIES

THE HIGH CONTRACTING PARTIES,

CONSIDERING that, in accordance with Article 40 of the Statute of the European System of Central Banks and of the European Central Bank and Article 21 of the Statute of the European Monetary Institute, the European Central Bank and the European Monetary Institute shall enjoy in the territories of the Member States such privileges and immunities as are necessary for the performance of their tasks,

HAVE AGREED upon the following provisions, which shall be annexed to the Treaty establishing the European Community:

Sole Article

The Protocol on the Privileges and Immunities of the European Communities, annexed to the Treaty establishing a Single Council and a Single Commission of the European Communities, shall be supplemented by the following provisions:

'Article 23

This Protocol shall also apply to the European Central Bank, to the members of its organs and to its staff, without prejudice to the provisions of the Protocol on the Statute of the European System of Central Banks and the European Central Bank.

The European Central Bank shall, in addition, be exempt from any form of taxation or imposition of a like nature on the occasion of any increase in its capital and from the various formalities which may be connected therewith in the State where the Bank has its seat. The activities of the Bank and of its organs carried on in accordance with the Statute of the European System of Central Banks and of the European Central Bank shall not be subject to any turnover tax.

The above provisions shall also apply to the European Monetary Institute. Its dissolution or liquidation shall not give rise to any imposition.'

PROTOCOL

ON DENMARK

THE HIGH CONTRACTING PARTIES,

DESIRING to settle certain particular problems relating to Denmark,

HAVE AGREED upon the following provisions, which shall be annexed to the Treaty establishing the European Community:

The provisions of Article 14 of the Protocol on the Statute of the European System of Central Banks and of the European Central Bank shall not affect the right of the National Bank of Denmark to carry out its existing tasks concerning those parts of the Kingdom of Denmark which are not part of the Community.

PROTOCOL
ON PORTUGAL

THE HIGH CONTRACTING PARTIES,

DESIRING to settle certain particular problems relating to Portugal,

HAVE AGREED upon the following provisions, which shall be annexed to the Treaty establishing the European Community:

1. Portugal is hereby authorized to maintain the facility afforded to the Autonomous Regions of the Azores and Madeira to benefit from an interest-free credit facility with the Banco de Portugal under the terms established by existing Portuguese law.

2. Portugal commits itself to pursue its best endeavours in order to put an end to the abovementioned facility as soon as possible.

PROTOCOL

ON THE TRANSITION TO THE THIRD STAGE OF ECONOMIC AND MONETARY UNION

THE HIGH CONTRACTING PARTIES,

Declare the irreversible character of the Community's movement to the third stage of economic and monetary union by signing the new Treaty provisions on economic and monetary union.

Therefore all Member States shall, whether they fulfil the necessary conditions for the adoption of a single currency or not, respect the will for the Community to enter swiftly into the third stage, and therefore no Member State shall prevent the entering into the third stage.

If by the end of 1997 the date of the beginning of the third stage has not been set, the Member States concerned, the Community institutions and other bodies involved shall expedite all preparatory work during 1998, in order to enable the Community to enter the third stage irrevocably on 1 January 1999 and to enable the ECB and the ESCB to start their full functioning from this date.

This Protocol shall be annexed to the Treaty establishing the European Community.

PROTOCOL

ON CERTAIN PROVISIONS RELATING TO THE UNITED KINGDOM OF GREAT BRITAIN AND NORTHERN IRELAND

THE HIGH CONTRACTING PARTIES,

RECOGNIZING that the United Kingdom shall not be obliged or committed to move to the third stage of economic and monetary union without a separate decision to do so by its government and Parliament,

NOTING the practice of the government of the United Kingdom to fund its borrowing requirement by the sale of debt to the private sector,

HAVE AGREED the following provisions, which shall be annexed to the Treaty establishing the European Community:

1. The United Kingdom shall notify the Council whether it intends to move to the third stage before the Council makes its assessment under Article 109j(2) of this Treaty.

   Unless the United Kingdom notifies the Council that it intends to move to the third stage, it shall be under no obligation to do so.

   If no date is set for the beginning of the third stage under Article 109j(3) of this Treaty, the United Kingdom may notify its intention to move to the third stage before 1 January 1998.

2. Paragraphs 3 to 9 shall have effect if the United Kingdom notifies the Council that it does not intend to move to the third stage.

3. The United Kingdom shall not be included among the majority of Member States which fulfil the necessary conditions referred to in the second indent of Article 109j(2) and the first indent of Article 109j(3) of this Treaty.

4. The United Kingdom shall retain its powers in the field of monetary policy according to national law.

5. Articles 3a(2), 104c(1), (9) and (11), 105(1) to (5), 105a, 107, 108, 108a, 109, 109a(1) and (2)(b) and 109l(4) and (5) of this Treaty shall not apply to the United Kingdom. In these provisions references to the Community or the Member States shall not include the United Kingdom and references to national central banks shall not include the Bank of England.

6. Articles 109e(4) and 109h and i of this Treaty shall continue to apply to the United Kingdom. Articles 109c(4) and 109m shall apply to the United Kingdom as if it had a derogation.

7. The voting rights of the United Kingdom shall be suspended in respect of acts of the Council referred to in the Articles listed in paragraph 5. For this purpose the weighted votes of the United Kingdom shall be excluded from any calculation of a qualified majority under Article 109k(5) of this Treaty.

   The United Kingdom shall also have no right to participate in the appointment of the President, the Vice-President and the other members of the Executive Board of the ECB under Articles 109a(2)(b) and 109*l*(1) of this Treaty.

8. Articles 3, 4, 6, 7, 9.2, 10.1, 10.3, 11.2, 12.1, 14, 16, 18 to 20, 22, 23, 26, 27, 30 to 34, 50 and 52 of the Protocol on the Statute of the European System of Central Banks and of the European Central Bank ('the Statute') shall not apply to the United Kingdom.

   In those Articles, references to the Community or the Member States shall not include the United Kingdom and references to national central banks or shareholders shall not include the Bank of England.

   References in Articles 10.3 and 30.2 of the Statute to 'subscribed capital of the ECB' shall not include capital subscribed by the Bank of England.

9. Article 109*l*(3) of this Treaty and Articles 44 to 48 of the Statute shall have effect, whether or not there is any Member State with a derogation, subject to the following amendments:

   (a) References in Article 44 to the tasks of the ECB and the EMI shall include those tasks that still need to be performed in the third stage owing to any decision of the United Kingdom not to move to that stage.

   (b) In addition to the tasks referred to in Article 47 the ECB shall also give advice in relation to and contribute to the preparation of any decision of the Council with regard to the United Kingdom taken in accordance with paragraphs 10(a) and 10(c).

   (c) The Bank of England shall pay up its subscription to the capital of the ECB as a contribution to its operational costs on the same basis as national central banks of Member States with a derogation.

10. If the United Kingdom does not move to the third stage, it may change its notification at any time after the beginning of that stage. In that event:

   (a) The United Kingdom shall have the right to move to the third stage provided only that it satisfies the necessary conditions. The Council, acting at the request of the United Kingdom and under the conditions and in accordance with the procedure laid down in Article 109k(2) of this Treaty, shall decide whether it fulfils the necessary conditions.

   (b) The Bank of England shall pay up its subscribed capital, transfer to the ECB foreign reserve assets and contribute to its reserves on the same basis as the national central bank of a Member State whose derogation has been abrogated.

   (c) The Council, acting under the conditions and in accordance with the procedure laid down in Article 109l(5) of this Treaty, shall take all other necessary decisions to enable the United Kingdom to move to the third stage.

   If the United Kingdom moves to the third stage pursuant to the provisions of this Protocol, paragraphs 3 to 9 shall cease to have effect.

11. Notwithstanding Articles 104 and 109e(3) of this Treaty and Article 21.1 of the Statute, the government of the United Kingdom may maintain its 'ways and means' facility with the Bank of England if and so long as the United Kingdom does not move to the third stage.

PROTOCOL

ON CERTAIN PROVISIONS
RELATING TO DENMARK

THE HIGH CONTRACTING PARTIES,

DESIRING to settle, in accordance with the general objectives of the Treaty establishing the European Community, certain particular problems existing at the present time,

TAKING INTO ACCOUNT that the Danish Constitution contains provisions which may imply a referendum in Denmark prior to Danish participation in the third stage of economic and monetary union,

HAVE AGREED on the following provisions, which shall be annexed to the Treaty establishing the European Community:

1. The Danish Government shall notify the Council of its position concerning participation in the third stage before the Council makes its assessment under Article 109j(2) of this Treaty.

2. In the event of a notification that Denmark will not participate in the third stage, Denmark shall have an exemption. The effect of the exemption shall be that all Articles and provisions of this Treaty and the Statute of the ESCB referring to a derogation shall be applicable to Denmark.

3. In such case, Denmark shall not be included among the majority of Member States which fulfil the necessary conditions referred to in the second indent of Article 109j(2) and the first indent of Article 109j(3) of this Treaty.

4. As for the abrogation of the exemption, the procedure referred to in Article 109k(2) shall only be initiated at the request of Denmark.

5. In the event of abrogation of the exemption status, the provisions of this Protocol shall cease to apply.

PROTOCOL

ON FRANCE

THE HIGH CONTRACTING PARTIES,

DESIRING to take into account a particular point relating to France,

HAVE AGREED upon the following provisions, which shall be annexed to the Treaty establishing the European Community:

France will keep the privilege of monetary emission in its overseas territories under the terms established by its national laws, and will be solely entitled to determine the parity of the CFP franc.

PROTOCOL

ON SOCIAL POLICY

THE HIGH CONTRACTING PARTIES,

NOTING that 11 Member States, that is to say the Kingdom of Belgium, the Kingdom of Denmark, the Federal Republic of Germany, the Hellenic Republic, the Kingdom of Spain, the French Republic, Ireland, the Italian Republic, the Grand Duchy of Luxembourg, the Kingdom of the Netherlands and the Portuguese Republic, wish to continue along the path laid down in the 1989 Social Charter; that they have adopted among themselves an Agreement to this end; that this Agreement is annexed to this Protocol; that this Protocol and the said Agreement are without prejudice to the provisions of this Treaty, particularly those relating to social policy which constitute an integral part of the *acquis communautaire:*

1. Agree to authorize those 11 Member States to have recourse to the institutions, procedures and mechanisms of the Treaty for the purposes of taking among themselves and applying as far as they are concerned the acts and decisions required for giving effect to the abovementioned Agreement.

2. The United Kingdom of Great Britain and Northern Ireland shall not take part in the deliberations and the adoption by the Council of Commission proposals made on the basis of this Protocol and the abovementioned Agreement.

   By way of derogation from Article 148(2) of the Treaty, acts of the Council which are made pursuant to this Protocol and which must be adopted by a qualified majority shall be deemed to be so adopted if they have received at least 44 votes in favour. The unanimity of the members of the Council, with the exception of the United Kingdom of Great Britain and Northern Ireland, shall be necessary for acts of the Council which must be adopted unanimously and for those amending the Commission proposal.

   Acts adopted by the Council and any financial consequences other than administrative costs entailed for the institutions shall not be applicable to the United Kingdom of Great Britain and Northern Ireland.

3. This Protocol shall be annexed to the Treaty establishing the European Community.

AGREEMENT

ON SOCIAL POLICY CONCLUDED BETWEEN THE MEMBER STATES OF THE EUROPEAN COMMUNITY WITH THE EXCEPTION OF THE UNITED KINGDOM OF GREAT BRITAIN AND NORTHERN IRELAND

The undersigned 11 HIGH CONTRACTING PARTIES, that is to say the Kingdom of Belgium, the Kingdom of Denmark, the Federal Republic of Germany, the Hellenic Republic, the Kingdom of Spain, the French Republic, Ireland, the Italian Republic, the Grand Duchy of Luxembourg, the Kingdom of the Netherlands and the Portuguese Republic (hereinafter referred to as 'the Member States'),

WISHING to implement the 1989 Social Charter on the basis of the *acquis communautaire,*

CONSIDERING the Protocol on social policy,

HAVE AGREED as follows:

Article 1

The Community and the Member States shall have as their objectives the promotion of employment, improved living and working conditions, proper social protection, dialogue between management and labour, the development of human resources with a view to lasting high employment and the combating of exclusion. To this end the Community and the Member States shall implement measures which take account of the diverse forms of national practices, in particular in the field of contractual relations, and the need to maintain the competitiveness of the Community economy.

Article 2

1. With a view to achieving the objectives of Article 1, the Community shall support and complement the activities of the Member States in the following fields:

— improvement in particular of the working environment to protect workers' health and safety;

— working conditions;

— the information and consultation of workers;

— equality between men and women with regard to labour market opportunities and treatment at work;

— the integration of persons excluded from the labour market, without prejudice to Article 127 of the Treaty establishing the European Community (hereinafter referred to as 'the Treaty').

2. To this end, the Council may adopt, by means of directives, minimum requirements for gradual implementation, having regard to the conditions and technical rules obtaining in each of the Member States. Such directives shall avoid imposing administrative, financial and legal constraints in a way which would hold back the creation and development of small and medium-sized undertakings.

The Council shall act in accordance with the procedure referred to in Article 189c of the Treaty after consulting the Economic and Social Committee.

3. However, the Council shall act unanimously on a proposal from the Commission, after consulting the European Parliament and the Economic and Social Committee, in the following areas:

— social security and social protection of workers;

— protection of workers where their employment contract is terminated;

— representation and collective defence of the interests of workers and employers, including co-determination, subject to paragraph 6;

— conditions of employment for third-country nationals legally residing in Community territory;

— financial contributions for promotion of employment and job-creation, without prejudice to the provisions relating to the Social Fund.

4. A Member State may entrust management and labour, at their joint request, with the implementation of directives adopted pursuant to paragraphs 2 and 3.

In this case, it shall ensure that, no later than the date on which a directive must be transposed in accordance with Article 189, management and labour have introduced the necessary measures by agreement, the Member State concerned being required to take any necessary measure enabling it at any time to be in a position to guarantee the results imposed by that directive.

5. The provisions adopted pursuant to this Article shall not prevent any Member State from maintaining or introducing more stringent protective measures compatible with the Treaty.

6. The provisions of this Article shall not apply to pay, the right of association, the right to strike or the right to impose lock-outs.

Article 3

1. The Commission shall have the task of promoting the consultation of management and labour at Community level and shall take any relevant measure to facilitate their dialogue by ensuring balanced support for the parties.

2. To this end, before submitting proposals in the social policy field, the Commission shall consult management and labour on the possible direction of Community action.

3. If, after such consultation, the Commission considers Community action advisable, it shall consult management and labour on the content of the envisaged proposal. Management and labour shall forward to the Commission an opinion or, where appropriate, a recommendation.

4. On the occasion of such consultation, management and labour may inform the Commission of their wish to initiate the process provided for in Article 4. The duration of the procedure shall not exceed nine months, unless the management and labour concerned and the Commission decide jointly to extend it.

Article 4

1. Should management and labour so desire, the dialogue between them at Community level may lead to contractual relations, including agreements.

2. Agreements concluded at Community level shall be implemented either in accordance with the procedures and practices specific to management and labour and the Member States or, in matters covered by Article 2, at the joint request of the signatory parties, by a Council decision on a proposal from the Commission.

The Council shall act by qualified majority, except where the agreement in question contains one or more provisions relating to one of the areas referred to in Article 2(3), in which case it shall act unanimously.

Article 5

With a view to achieving the objectives of Article 1 and without prejudice to the other provisions of the Treaty, the Commission shall encourage cooperation between the Member States and facilitate the coordination of their action in all social policy fields under this Agreement.

Article 6

1. Each Member State shall ensure that the principle of equal pay for male and female workers for equal work is applied.

2. For the purpose of this Article, 'pay' means the ordinary basic or minimum wage or salary and any other consideration, whether in cash or in kind, which the worker receives directly or indirectly, in respect of his employment, from his employer.

Equal pay without discrimination based on sex means:

(a) that pay for the same work at piece rates shall be calculated on the basis of the same unit of measurement;

(b) that pay for work at time rates shall be the same for the same job.

3. This Article shall not prevent any Member State from maintaining or adopting measures providing for specific advantages in order to make it easier for women to pursue a vocational activity or to prevent or compensate for disadvantages in their professional careers.

Article 7

The Commission shall draw up a report each year on progress in achieving the objectives of Article 1, including the demographic situation in the Community. It shall forward the report to the European Parliament, the Council and the Economic and Social Committee.

The European Parliament may invite the Commission to draw up reports on particular problems concerning the social situation.

DECLARATIONS

1. Declaration on Article 2(2)

The 11 High Contracting Parties note that in the discussions on Article 2(2) of the Agreement it was agreed that the Community does not intend, in laying down minimum requirements for the protection of the safety and health of employees, to discriminate in a manner unjustified by the circumstances against employees in small and medium-sized undertakings.

2. Declaration on Article 4(2)

The 11 High Contracting Parties declare that the first of the arrangements for application of the agreements between management and labour at Community level — referred to in Article 4(2) — will consist in developing, by collective bargaining according to the rules of each Member State, the content of the agreements, and that consequently this arrangement implies no obligation on the Member States to apply the agreements directly or to work out rules for their transposition, nor any obligation to amend national legislation in force to facilitate their implementation.

PROTOCOL

ON ECONOMIC AND SOCIAL COHESION

THE HIGH CONTRACTING PARTIES,

RECALLING that the Union has set itself the objective of promoting economic and social progress, *inter alia,* through the strengthening of economic and social cohesion,

RECALLING that Article 2 of the Treaty establishing the European Community includes the task of promoting economic and social cohesion and solidarity between Member States and that the strengthening of economic and social cohesion figures among the activities of the Community listed in Article 3,

RECALLING that the provisions of Part Three, Title XIV, on economic and social cohesion as a whole provide the legal basis for consolidating and further developing the Community's action in the field of economic and social cohesion, including the creation of a new fund,

RECALLING that the provisions of Part Three, Title XII on trans-European networks and Title XVI on environment envisage a Cohesion Fund to be set up before 31 December 1993,

STATING their belief that progress towards economic and monetary union will contribute to the economic growth of all Member States,

NOTING that the Community's structural Funds are being doubled in real terms between 1987 and 1993, implying large transfers, especially as a proportion of GDP of the less prosperous Member States,

NOTING that the European Investment Bank is lending large and increasing amounts for the benefit of the poorer regions,

NOTING the desire for greater flexibility in the arrangements for allocations from the structural Funds,

NOTING the desire for modulation of the levels of Community participation in programmes and projects in certain countries,

NOTING the proposal to take greater account of the relative prosperity of Member States in the system of own resources,

REAFFIRM that the promotion of economic and social cohesion is vital to the full development and enduring success of the Community, and underline the importance of the inclusion of economic and social cohesion in Articles 2 and 3 of this Treaty,

REAFFIRM their conviction that the structural Funds should continue to play a considerable part in the achievement of Community objectives in the field of cohesion,

REAFFIRM their conviction that the European Investment Bank should continue to devote the majority of its resources to the promotion of economic and social cohesion, and declare their willingness to review the capital needs of the European Investment Bank as soon as this is necessary for that purpose,

REAFFIRM the need for a thorough evaluation of the operation and effectiveness of the structural Funds in 1992, and the need to review, on that occasion, the appropriate size of these Funds in the light of the tasks of the Community in the area of economic and social cohesion,

AGREE that the Cohesion Fund to be set up before 31 December 1993 will provide Community financial contributions to projects in the fields of environment and trans-European networks in Member States with a per capita GNP of less than 90% of the Community average which have a programme leading to the fulfilment of the conditions of economic convergence as set out in Article 104c,

DECLARE their intention of allowing a greater margin of flexibility in allocating financing from the structural Funds to specific needs not covered under the present structural Funds regulations,

DECLARE their willingness to modulate the levels of Community participation in the context of programmes and projects of the structural Funds, with a view to avoiding excessive increases in budgetary expenditure in the less prosperous Member States,

RECOGNIZE the need to monitor regularly the progress made towards achieving economic and social cohesion and state their willingness to study all necessary measures in this respect,

DECLARE their intention of taking greater account of the contributive capacity of individual Member States in the system of own resources, and of examining means of correcting, for the less prosperous Member States, regressive elements existing in the present own resources system,

AGREE to annex this Protocol to the Treaty establishing the European Community.

PROTOCOL

ON THE ECONOMIC AND SOCIAL COMMITTEE AND THE COMMITTEE OF THE REGIONS

THE HIGH CONTRACTING PARTIES,

HAVE AGREED upon the following provision, which shall be annexed to this Treaty establishing the European Community:

The Economic and Social Committee and the Committee of the Regions shall have a common organizational structure.

PROTOCOL

ANNEXED TO THE TREATY ON EUROPEAN UNION AND TO THE TREATIES ESTABLISHING THE EUROPEAN COMMUNITIES

THE HIGH CONTRACTING PARTIES,

HAVE AGREED upon the following provision, which shall be annexed to the Treaty on European Union and to the Treaties establishing the European Communities:

Nothing in the Treaty on European Union, or in the Treaties establishing the European Communities, or in the Treaties or Acts modifying or supplementing those Treaties, shall affect the application in Ireland of Article 40.3.3. of the Constitution of Ireland.

FINAL ACT

1. The Conferences of the Representatives of the Governments of the Member States convened in Rome on 15 December 1990 to adopt by common accord the amendments to be made to the Treaty establishing the European Economic Community with a view to the achievement of political union and with a view to the final stages of economic and monetary union, and those convened in Brussels on 3 February 1992 with a view to amending the Treaties establishing respectively the European Coal and Steel Community and the European Atomic Energy Community as a result of the amendments envisaged for the Treaty establishing the European Economic Community have adopted the following texts:

I.

THE TREATY ON EUROPEAN UNION

II.

PROTOCOLS

1. Protocol on the acquisition of property in Denmark

2. Protocol concerning Article 119 of the Treaty establishing the European Community

3. Protocol on the Statute of the European System of Central Banks and of the European Central Bank

4. Protocol on the Statute of the European Monetary Institute

5. Protocol on the excessive deficit procedure

6. Protocol on the convergence criteria referred to in Article 109j of the Treaty establishing the European Community

7. Protocol amending the Protocol on the privileges and immunities of the European Communities

8. Protocol on Denmark

9. Protocol on Portugal

10. Protocol on the transition to the third stage of economic and monetary union

11. Protocol on certain provisions relating to the United Kingdom of Great Britain and Northern Ireland

12. Protocol on certain provisions relating to Denmark

13. Protocol on France

14. Protocol on social policy, to which is annexed an agreement concluded between the Member States of the European Community with the exception of the United Kingdom of Great Britain and Northern Ireland, to which two declarations are attached

15. Protocol on economic and social cohesion

16. Protocol on the Economic and Social Committee and the Committee of the Regions

17. Protocol annexed to the Treaty on European Union and to the Treaties establishing the European Communities

The Conferences agreed that the Protocols referred to in 1 to 16 above will be annexed to the Treaty establishing the European Community and that the Protocol referred to in 17 above will be annexed to the Treaty on European Union and to the Treaties establishing the European Communities.

2. At the time of signature of these texts, the Conferences adopted the declarations listed below and annexed to this Final Act:

III.

DECLARATIONS

1. Declaration on civil protection, energy and tourism

2. Declaration on nationality of a Member State

3. Declaration on Part Three, Titles III and VI, of the Treaty establishing the European Community

4. Declaration on Part Three, Title VI, of the Treaty establishing the European Community

5. Declaration on monetary cooperation with non-Community countries

6. Declaration on monetary relations with the Republic of San Marino, the Vatican City and the Principality of Monaco

7. Declaration on Article 73d of the Treaty establishing the European Community

8. Declaration on Article 109 of the Treaty establishing the European Community

30. Declaration on Western European Union

31. Declaration on asylum

32. Declaration on police cooperation

33. Declaration on disputes between the ECB and the EMI and their servants

Done at Maastricht this seventh day of February in the year one thousand nine hundred and ninety-two.

DECLARATION

ON CIVIL PROTECTION, ENERGY AND TOURISM

The Conference declares that the question of introducing into the Treaty establishing the European Community Titles relating to the spheres referred to in Article 3(t) of that Treaty will be examined, in accordance with the procedure laid down in Article N(2) of the Treaty on European Union, on the basis of a report which the Commission will submit to the Council by 1996 at the latest.

The Commission declares that Community action in those spheres will be pursued on the basis of the present provisions of the Treaties establishing the European Communities.

DECLARATION

ON NATIONALITY OF A MEMBER STATE

The Conference declares that, wherever in the Treaty establishing the European Community reference is made to nationals of the Member States, the question whether an individual possesses the nationality of a Member State shall be settled solely by reference to the national law of the Member State concerned. Member States may declare, for information, who are to be considered their nationals for Community purposes by way of a declaration lodged with the Presidency and may amend any such declaration when necessary.

DECLARATION

ON PART THREE, TITLES III AND VI, OF THE TREATY ESTABLISHING THE EUROPEAN COMMUNITY

The Conference affirms that, for the purposes of applying the provisions set out in Part Three, Title III, Chapter 4 on capital and payments, and Title VI on economic and monetary policy, of this Treaty, the usual practice, according to which the Council meets in the composition of Economic and Finance Ministers, shall be continued, without prejudice to Article 109j(2) to (4) and Article 109k(2).

DECLARATION

ON PART THREE, TITLE VI, OF THE TREATY ESTABLISHING THE EUROPEAN COMMUNITY

The Conference affirms that the President of the European Council shall invite the Economic and Finance Ministers to participate in European Council meetings when the European Council is discussing matters relating to economic and monetary union.

DECLARATION

ON MONETARY COOPERATION WITH NON-COMMUNITY COUNTRIES

The Conference affirms that the Community shall aim to contribute to stable international monetary relations. To this end the Community shall be prepared to cooperate with other European countries and with those non-European countries with which the Community has close economic ties.

DECLARATION

ON MONETARY RELATIONS WITH THE REPUBLIC OF SAN MARINO, THE VATICAN CITY AND THE PRINCIPALITY OF MONACO

The Conference agrees that the existing monetary relations between Italy and San Marino and the Vatican City and between France and Monaco remain unaffected by the Treaty establishing the European Community until the introduction of the ecu as the single currency of the Community.

The Community undertakes to facilitate such renegotiations of existing arrangements as might become necessary as a result of the introduction of the ecu as a single currency.

DECLARATION

ON ARTICLE 73d OF THE TREATY
ESTABLISHING THE EUROPEAN COMMUNITY

The Conference affirms that the right of Member States to apply the relevant provisions of their tax law as referred to in Article 73d(1)(a) of this Treaty will apply only with respect to the relevant provisions which exist at the end of 1993. However, this Declaration shall apply only to capital movements between Member States and to payments effected between Member States.

DECLARATION

ON ARTICLE 109 OF THE TREATY ESTABLISHING THE EUROPEAN COMMUNITY

The Conference emphasizes that use of the term 'formal agreements' in Article 109(1) is not intended to create a new category of international agreement within the meaning of Community law.

DECLARATION

ON PART THREE, TITLE XVI, OF THE TREATY ESTABLISHING THE EUROPEAN COMMUNITY

The Conference considers that, in view of the increasing importance of nature conservation at national, Community and international level, the Community should, in exercising its powers under the provisions of Part Three, Title XVI, take account of the specific requirements of this area.

DECLARATION

ON ARTICLES 109, 130r AND 130y OF THE TREATY ESTABLISHING THE EUROPEAN COMMUNITY

The Conference considers that the provisions of Article 109(5), Article 130r(4), second subparagraph, and Article 130y do not affect the principles resulting from the judgment handed down by the Court of Justice in the AETR case.

DECLARATION

ON THE DIRECTIVE OF 24 NOVEMBER 1988
(Emissions)

The Conference declares that changes in Community legislation cannot undermine the derogations granted to Spain and Portugal until 31 December 1999 under the Council Directive of 24 November 1988 on the limitation of emissions of certain pollutants into the air from large combustion plants.

DECLARATION
ON THE EUROPEAN DEVELOPMENT FUND

The Conference agrees that the European Development Fund will continue to be financed by national contributions in accordance with the current provisions.

DECLARATION

ON THE ROLE OF NATIONAL PARLIAMENTS
IN THE EUROPEAN UNION

The Conference considers that it is important to encourage greater involvement of national parliaments in the activities of the European Union.

To this end, the exchange of information between national parliaments and the European Parliament should be stepped up. In this context, the governments of the Member States will ensure, *inter alia,* that national parliaments receive Commission proposals for legislation in good time for information or possible examination.

Similarly, the Conference considers that it is important for contacts between the national parliaments and the European Parliament to be stepped up, in particular through the granting of appropriate reciprocal facilities and regular meetings between members of Parliament interested in the same issues.

DECLARATION

ON THE CONFERENCE OF THE PARLIAMENTS

The Conference invites the European Parliament and the national parliaments to meet as necessary as a Conference of the Parliaments (or 'assises').

The Conference of the Parliaments will be consulted on the main features of the European Union, without prejudice to the powers of the European Parliament and the rights of the national parliaments. The President of the European Council and the President of the Commission will report to each session of the Conference of the Parliaments on the state of the Union.

DECLARATION

ON THE NUMBER OF MEMBERS OF THE COMMISSION AND OF THE EUROPEAN PARLIAMENT

The Conference agrees that the Member States will examine the questions relating to the number of members of the Commission and the number of members of the European Parliament no later than at the end of 1992, with a view to reaching an agreement which will permit the establishment of the necessary legal basis for fixing the number of members of the European Parliament in good time for the 1994 elections. The decisions will be taken in the light, *inter alia,* of the need to establish the overall size of the European Parliament in an enlarged Community.

DECLARATION

ON THE HIERARCHY OF COMMUNITY ACTS

The Conference agrees that the Intergovernmental Conference to be convened in 1996 will examine to what extent it might be possible to review the classification of Community acts with a view to establishing an appropriate hierarchy between the different categories of act.

DECLARATION

ON THE RIGHT OF ACCESS TO INFORMATION

The Conference considers that transparency of the decision-making process strengthens the democratic nature of the institutions and the public's confidence in the administration. The Conference accordingly recommends that the Commission submit to the Council no later than 1993 a report on measures designed to improve public access to the information available to the institutions.

DECLARATION

ON ESTIMATED COSTS UNDER COMMISSION PROPOSALS

The Conference notes that the Commission undertakes, by basing itself where appropriate on any consultations it considers necessary and by strengthening its system for evaluating Community legislation, to take account in its legislative proposals of costs and benefits to the Member States' public authorities and all the parties concerned.

DECLARATION

ON THE IMPLEMENTATION OF COMMUNITY LAW

1. The Conference stresses that it is central to the coherence and unity of the process of European construction that each Member State should fully and accurately transpose into national law the Community Directives addressed to it within the deadlines laid down therein.

   Moreover, the Conference, while recognizing that it must be for each Member State to determine how the provisions of Community law can best be enforced in the light of its own particular institutions, legal system and other circumstances, but in any event in compliance with Article 189 of the Treaty establishing the European Community, considers it essential for the proper functioning of the Community that the measures taken by the different Member States should result in Community law being applied with the same effectiveness and rigour as in the application of their national law.

2. The Conference calls on the Commission to ensure, in exercising its powers under Article 155 of this Treaty, that Member States fulfil their obligations. It asks the Commission to publish periodically a full report for the Member States and the European Parliament.

DECLARATION

ON ASSESSMENT OF THE ENVIRONMENTAL IMPACT OF COMMUNITY MEASURES

The Conference notes that the Commission undertakes in its proposals, and that the Member States undertake in implementing those proposals, to take full account of their environmental impact and of the principle of sustainable growth.

DECLARATION

ON THE COURT OF AUDITORS

The Conference emphasizes the special importance it attaches to the task assigned to the Court of Auditors by Articles 188a, 188b, 188c and 206 of the Treaty establishing the European Community.

It requests the other Community institutions to consider, together with the Court of Auditors, all appropriate ways of enhancing the effectiveness of its work.

DECLARATION

ON THE ECONOMIC AND SOCIAL COMMITTEE

The Conference agrees that the Economic and Social Committee will enjoy the same independence with regard to its budget and staff management as the Court of Auditors has enjoyed hitherto.

DECLARATION

ON COOPERATION WITH CHARITABLE ASSOCIATIONS

The Conference stresses the importance, in pursuing the objectives of Article 117 of the Treaty establishing the European Community, of cooperation between the latter and charitable associations and foundations as institutions responsible for social welfare establishments and services.

DECLARATION

ON THE PROTECTION OF ANIMALS

The Conference calls upon the European Parliament, the Council and the Commission, as well as the Member States, when drafting and implementing Community legislation on the common agricultural policy, transport, the internal market and research, to pay full regard to the welfare requirements of animals.

DECLARATION

ON THE REPRESENTATION OF THE INTERESTS
OF THE OVERSEAS COUNTRIES AND TERRITORIES
REFERRED TO IN
ARTICLE 227(3) AND (5)(a) AND (b)
OF THE TREATY ESTABLISHING THE
EUROPEAN COMMUNITY

The Conference, noting that in exceptional circumstances divergences may arise between the interests of the Union and those of the overseas countries and territories referred to in Article 227(3) and (5)(a) and (b), agrees that the Council will seek to reach a solution which accords with the position of the Union. However, in the event that this proves impossible, the Conference agrees that the Member State concerned may act separately in the interests of the said overseas countries and territories, without this affecting the Community's interests. The Member State concerned will give notice to the Council and the Commission where such a divergence of interests is likely to occur and, when separate action proves unavoidable, make it clear that it is acting in the interests of an overseas territory mentioned above.

This declaration also applies to Macao and East Timor.

DECLARATION

ON THE OUTERMOST REGIONS OF THE COMMUNITY

The Conference acknowledges that the outermost regions of the Community (the French overseas departments, Azores and Madeira and Canary Islands) suffer from major structural backwardness compounded by several phenomena (remoteness, island status, small size, difficult topography and climate, economic dependence on a few products), the permanence and combination of which severely restrain their economic and social development.

It considers that, while the provisions of the Treaty establishing the European Community and secondary legislation apply automatically to the outermost regions, it is none the less possible to adopt specific measures to assist them inasmuch and as long as there is an objective need to take such measures with a view to the economic and social development of those regions. Such measures should have as their aim both the completion of the internal market and a recognition of the regional reality to enable the outermost regions to achieve the average economic and social level of the Community.

DECLARATION

ON VOTING IN THE FIELD OF THE COMMON FOREIGN AND SECURITY POLICY

The Conference agrees that, with regard to Council decisions requiring unanimity, Member States will, to the extent possible, avoid preventing a unanimous decision where a qualified majority exists in favour of that decision.

DECLARATION

ON PRACTICAL ARRANGEMENTS IN THE FIELD OF THE COMMON FOREIGN AND SECURITY POLICY

The Conference agrees that the division of work between the Political Committee and the Committee of Permanent Representatives will be examined at a later stage, as will the practical arrangements for merging the Political Cooperation Secretariat with the General Secretariat of the Council and for cooperation between the latter and the Commission.

DECLARATION

ON THE USE OF LANGUAGES IN THE FIELD OF THE COMMON FOREIGN AND SECURITY POLICY

The Conference agrees that the use of languages shall be in accordance with the rules of the European Communities.

For Coreu communications, the current practice of European political cooperation will serve as a guide for the time being.

All common foreign and security policy texts which are submitted to or adopted at meetings of the European Council and of the Council as well as all texts which are to be published are immediately and simultaneously translated into all the official Community languages.

DECLARATION

ON WESTERN EUROPEAN UNION

The Conference notes the following declarations:

I. DECLARATION

by Belgium, Germany, Spain, France, Italy, Luxembourg, the Netherlands, Portugal and the United Kingdom of Great Britain and Northern Ireland, which are members of the Western European Union and also members of the European Union
on
THE ROLE OF THE WESTERN EUROPEAN UNION
AND ITS RELATIONS
WITH THE EUROPEAN UNION AND WITH THE ATLANTIC ALLIANCE

Introduction

1. WEU Member States agree on the need to develop a genuine European security and defence identity and a greater European responsibility on defence matters. This identity will be pursued through a gradual process involving successive phases. WEU will form an integral part of the process of the development of the European Union and will enhance its contribution to solidarity within the Atlantic Alliance. WEU Member States agree to strengthen the role of WEU, in the longer term perspective of a common defence policy within the European Union which might in time lead to a common defence, compatible with that of the Atlantic Alliance.

2. WEU will be developed as the defence component of the European Union and as a means to strengthen the European pillar of the Atlantic Alliance. To this end, it will formulate common European defence policy and carry forward its concrete implementation through the further development of its own operational role.

WEU Member States take note of Article J.4 relating to the common foreign and security policy of the Treaty on European Union which reads as follows:

'1. The common foreign and security policy shall include all questions related to the security of the Union, including the eventual framing of a common defence policy, which might in time lead to a common defence.

2. The Union requests the Western European Union (WEU), which is an integral part of the development of the Union, to elaborate and implement decisions and actions of the Union which have defence implications. The Council shall, in agreement with the institutions of the WEU, adopt the necessary practical arrangements.

3. Issues having defence implications dealt with under this Article shall not be subject to the procedures set out in Article J.3.

4. The policy of the Union in accordance with this Article shall not prejudice the specific character of the security and defence policy of certain Member States and shall respect the obligations of certain Member States under the North Atlantic Treaty and be compatible with the common security and defence policy established within that framework.

5. The provisions of this Article shall not prevent the development of closer cooperation between two or more Member States on a bilateral level, in the framework of the WEU and the Atlantic Alliance, provided such cooperation does not run counter to or impede that provided for in this Title.

6. With a view to furthering the objective of this Treaty, and having in view the date of 1998 in the context of Article XII of the Brussels Treaty, the provisions of this Article may be revised as provided for in Article N(2) on the basis of a report to be presented in 1996 by the Council to the European Council, which shall include an evaluation of the progress made and the experience gained until then.'

A — WEU's relations with European Union

3. The objective is to build up WEU in stages as the defence component of the European Union. To this end, WEU is prepared, at the request of the European Union, to elaborate and implement decisions and actions of the Union which have defence implications.

To this end, WEU will take the following measures to develop a close working relationship with the Union:

— as appropriate, synchronization of the dates and venues of meetings and harmonization of working methods;

— establishment of close cooperation between the Council and Secretariat-General of WEU on the one hand, and the Council of the Union and General Secretariat of the Council on the other;

— consideration of the harmonization of the sequence and duration of the respective Presidencies;

— arranging for appropriate modalities so as to ensure that the Commission of the European Communities is regularly informed and, as appropriate, consulted on

WEU activities in accordance with the role of the Commission in the common foreign and security policy as defined in the Treaty on European Union;

— encouragement of closer cooperation between the Parliamentary Assembly of WEU and the European Parliament.

The WEU Council shall, in agreement with the competent bodies of the European Union, adopt the necessary practical arrangements.

B — WEU's relations with the Atlantic Alliance

4. The objective is to develop WEU as a means to strengthen the European pillar of the Atlantic Alliance. Accordingly WEU is prepared to develop further the close working links between WEU and the Alliance and to strengthen the role, responsibilities and contributions of WEU Member States in the Alliance. This will be undertaken on the basis of the necessary transparency and complementarity between the emerging European security and defence identity and the Alliance. WEU will act in conformity with the positions adopted in the Atlantic Alliance.

— WEU Member States will intensify their coordination on Alliance issues which represent an important common interest with the aim of introducing joint positions agreed in WEU into the process of consultation in the Alliance which will remain the essential forum for consultation among its members and the venue for agreement on policies bearing on the security and defence commitments of Allies under the North Atlantic Treaty.

— Where necessary, dates and venues of meetings will be synchronized and working methods harmonized.

— Close cooperation will be established between the Secretariats-General of WEU and NATO.

C — Operational role of WEU

5. WEU's operational role will be strengthened by examining and defining appropriate missions, structures and means, covering in particular:

— WEU planning cell;

— closer military cooperation complementary to the Alliance in particular in the fields of logistics, transport, training and strategic surveillance;

— meetings of WEU Chiefs of Defence Staff;

— military units answerable to WEU.

Other proposals will be examined further, including:

— enhanced cooperation in the field of armaments with the aim of creating a European armaments agency;

— development of the WEU Institute into a European Security and Defence Academy.

Arrangements aimed at giving WEU a stronger operational role will be fully compatible with the military dispositions necessary to ensure the collective defence of all Allies.

D — Other measures

6. As a consequence of the measures set out above, and in order to facilitate the strengthening of WEU's role, the seat of the WEU Council and Secretariat will be transferred to Brussels.

7. Representation on the WEU Council must be such that the Council is able to exercise its functions continuously in accordance with Article VIII of the modified Brussels Treaty. Member States may draw on a double-hatting formula, to be worked out, consisting of their representatives to the Alliance and to the European Union.

8. WEU notes that, in accordance with the provisions of Article J.4(6) concerning the common foreign and security policy of the Treaty on European Union, the Union will decide to review the provisions of this Article with a view to furthering the objective to be set by it in accordance with the procedure defined. The WEU will re-examine the present provisions in 1996. This re-examination will take account of the progress and experience acquired and will extend to relations between WEU and the Atlantic Alliance.

II. DECLARATION

by Belgium, Germany, Spain, France, Italy, Luxembourg, the Netherlands, Portugal and the United Kingdom of Great Britain and Northern Ireland which are members of the Western European Union

'The Member States of WEU welcome the development of the European security and defence identity. They are determined, taking into account the role of WEU as the defence component of the European Union and as the means to strengthen the European pillar of the Atlantic Alliance, to put the relationship between WEU and the other European States on a new basis for the sake of stability and security in Europe. In this spirit, they propose the following:

States which are members of the European Union are invited to accede to WEU on conditions to be agreed in accordance with Article XI of the modified Brussels Treaty, or to become observers if they so wish. Simultaneously, other European Member States of NATO are invited to become associate members of WEU in a way which will give them the possibility of participating fully in the activities of WEU.

The Member States of WEU assume that treaties and agreements corresponding with the above proposals will be concluded before 31 December 1992.'

DECLARATION

ON ASYLUM

1. The Conference agrees that, in the context of the proceedings provided for in Articles K.1 and K.3 of the provisions on cooperation in the fields of justice and home affairs, the Council will consider as a matter of priority questions concerning Member States' asylum policies, with the aim of adopting, by the beginning of 1993, common action to harmonize aspects of them, in the light of the work programme and timetable contained in the report on asylum drawn up at the request of the European Council meeting in Luxembourg on 28 and 29 June 1991.

2. In this connection, the Council will also consider, by the end of 1993, on the basis of a report, the possibility of applying Article K.9 to such matters.

DECLARATION

ON POLICE COOPERATION

The Conference confirms the agreement of the Member States on the objectives underlying the German delegation's proposals at the European Council meeting in Luxembourg on 28 and 29 June 1991.

For the present, the Member States agree to examine as a matter of priority the drafts submitted to them, on the basis of the work programme and timetable agreed upon in the report drawn up at the request of the Luxembourg European Council, and they are willing to envisage the adoption of practical measures in areas such as those suggested by the German delegation, relating to the following functions in the exchange of information and experience:

— support for national criminal investigation and security authorities, in particular in the coordination of investigations and search operations;

— creation of databases;

— central analysis and assessment of information in order to take stock of the situation and identify investigative approaches;

— collection and analysis of national prevention programmes for forwarding to Member States and for drawing up Europe-wide prevention strategies;

— measures relating to further training, research, forensic matters and criminal records departments.

Member States agree to consider on the basis of a report, during 1994 at the latest, whether the scope of such cooperation should be extended.

DECLARATION

ON DISPUTES BETWEEN THE ECB AND THE EMI AND THEIR SERVANTS

The Conference considers it proper that the Court of First Instance should hear this class of action in accordance with Article 168a of the Treaty establishing the European Community. The Conference therefore invites the institutions to adapt the relevant rules accordingly.

Hecho en Maastricht, el siete de febrero de mil novecientos noventa y dos.

Udfærdiget i Maastricht, den syvende februar nitten hundrede og tooghalvfems.

Geschehen zu Maastricht am siebten Februar neunzehnhundertzweiundneunzig.

Έγινε στο Μάαστριχτ, στις εφτά Φεβρουαρίου χίλια εννιακόσια ενενήντα δύο.

Done at Maastricht on the seventh day of February in the year one thousand nine hundred and ninety-two.

Fait à Maastricht, le sept février mil neuf cent quatre-vingt-douze.

Arna dhéanamh i Maastricht, an seachtú lá d'Fheabhra, míle naoi gcéad nócha a dó.

Fatto a Maastricht, addì sette febbraio millenovecentonovantadue.

Gedaan te Maastricht, de zevende februari negentienhonderd twee-en-negentig.

Feito em Maastricht, em sete de Fevereiro de mil novecentos e noventa e dois.

Pour Sa Majesté le Roi des Belges
Voor Zijne Majesteit de Koning der Belgen

For Hendes Majestæt Danmarks Dronning

Für den Präsidenten der Bundesrepublik Deutschland

Για τον Πρόεδρο της Ελληνικής Δημοκρατίας

Por Su Majestad el Rey de España

Pour le Président de la République française

Thar ceann Uachtarán na hEireann
For the President of Ireland

Per il Presidente della Repubblica italiana

Pour Son Altesse Royale le Grand-Duc de Luxembourg

Voor Hare Majesteit de Koningin der Nederlanden

Pelo Presidente da República Portuguesa

For Her Majesty the Queen of the United Kingdom of Great Britain and Northern
Ireland

European Communities — Council

Treaty on European Union

Luxembourg: Office for Official Publications of the European Communities

1992 — 253 pp. — 17.6 × 25 cm

ISBN 92-824-0959-7

Price (excluding VAT) in Luxembourg: ECU 9